WRITTEN
COMMUNICATION

PENGUIN BOOKS

WRITTEN COMMUNICATION

· · · · · · · · · · · · · · · · · · ·

The essential guide to letter writing

NINA VALENTINE

PENGUIN BOOKS

Published by the Penguin Group
Penguin Group (Australia)
250 Camberwell Road, Camberwell, Victoria 3124, Australia
(a division of Pearson Australia Group Pty Ltd)

New York   Toronto   London   Dublin   New Delhi
Auckland   Johannesburg

Penguin Books Ltd, Registered Offices: 80 Strand, London, WC2R 0RL, England

First published as *The Compact Guide to Writing Letters*, by Nina Valentine,
Penguin Books Australia Ltd, 1994
This revised edition published by Penguin Group (Australia), 2007
Revisions and additional text by Victoria Heywood

10 9 8 7 6 5 4 3 2 1

Design by Elizabeth Theodosiadis © Penguin Group (Australia)
Cover photograph by Getty Images
Typeset in Grotesque by Sunset Digital Pty Ltd, Brisbane
Printed in Australia by McPhersons Printing Group, Maryborough, Victoria

National Library of Australia
Cataloguing-in-Publication data:

   Valentine, Nina.
   Written communication.
   ISBN-13: 978 0 14 3005766 (pbk.).
   ISBN-10: 0 14 3005766 (pbk.).
   1. Written communication. 2. English language - Written
   English. I. Title.

   808.06

www.penguin.com.au

Contents

Introduction

There are times when we all need to write – whether it's a handwritten letter to friends, a formal reply to an invitation, a business email, a job application, or a letter of complaint written on your computer. Quite simply, there is no substitute for the courtesy and permanency of the written word, despite the widespread use of the telephone and mobile phone in our personal and professional lives.

For many people, putting their thoughts down in writing can be a daunting task. However, the more you write, the easier it becomes. Knowing how to say things correctly and effectively can help streamline business correspondence, prevent misunderstandings and strengthen links with your family, friends and colleagues.

This book aims to give you all the help you need to express yourself clearly and get your message across. It includes samples of letters that are used in everyday situations, which you can adapt to suit your own circumstances and personal style. There are also helpful examples of what *not* to do. You'll be shown how to set out a business letter, how to word invitations, and how to address envelopes correctly with the right titles for the recipients.

We are now in the twenty-first century, and writing goes far beyond the traditional letter. Much communication is now done by email and fax, so this book also covers communication by these methods. Use this book as your guide, and enjoy the pleasure of being able to express yourself more confidently and clearly in writing.

1
Why Write?

Receiving a letter or email can be one of the great joys in life; so it must follow that writing is an exercise in giving joy to others? Well, not necessarily.

There are unpleasant communications – those of complaint or Dear John letters, for example. They bring anything but joy. But generally people like receiving letters, especially invitations or a family email packed with news, relating all the tiny events that make up the lives of its various members.

A letter or email brings with it part of the person who wrote it. Whether it was the intention or not, the personality of the writer takes life on the page, so that it is a little like having a conversation on paper or on your computer screen. You cannot speak to the writer there and then, but you can contemplate what they have written, re-read their words, and relate even more directly to the communicator.

When it is time to answer the letter or email, it is your turn to be the communicator. You can answer the questions put to you, and pose some of your own. You can express all the emotions and thoughts that were brought to the surface by the letter. And you can think before you write – not say in haste something that you may regret.

But before you pick up your pen or put a finger on your keyboard, think about your reason for writing. Do you really need or want to make a permanent statement? Is your message necessary? Would a telephone call be more appropriate? Who is your recipient? Would you be embarrassed to have this communication surface again in a year's time? If you decide that yes, you really do need to write, then continue.

Write or ring?

The greatest argument for a letter, fax or email, as opposed to a phone call, is that there is a permanent record of what has been said. A letter puts ideas and commitments on the page, and so long as it is not destroyed, it is there forever. This means that while you are likely to initiate and negotiate matters by phone, you will still clinch your deals in writing; it also means that while the phone has become the means of much personal communication, the big events – birth, marriage, bereavement, success, absence – should still be marked by a letter.

OCCASIONS FOR WRITING

There are numerous types of written communications for all kinds of occasions. Once you have decided that writing is the most effective way of getting your message across, you then need to consider how you will communicate – hand-written or computer-generated letter, fax or email.

Handwritten correspondence

Pen and ink is the traditional method of corresponding with people you know well, although email is rapidly taking over thanks to its speed and convenience. However, for important personal communication, a handwritten letter shows that you have taken time and trouble. (Just make sure that your handwriting is easily legible.)

Letters of encouragement or congratulation rate high on the scale of marvellous letters to receive. They may underline a success to come or one achieved, and can be cherished and appreciated for years to come. A phone call is good to receive too, but it does not have the power to move the receiver six months later, as a re-read letter can do. Such letters become keepsakes.

Letters of thanks for some service received are very important too. They bring with them a warm recollection of the occasion and are a welcome addition to a spoken 'thank you' at the time because they prove that the writer has again thought of the person involved and has wanted to express thanks once more.

Letters sent to someone recently bereaved can be among the most comforting things of all. To know that you are in someone else's thoughts at such a time brings an emotional response that is part of the healing process. Such letters are not always easy to write, but they rate so far above a sterile card that they are worth tackling.

Choose your materials carefully. Quality paper and a decent pen give a very different impression to a hastily scribbled note in biro on a flimsy sheet of paper. As a general rule, the heavier the paper, the better. Be wary of brightly coloured paper (unless you want to make a statement) or fussy designs. These can make it difficult for the recipient to decipher the contents of your letter.

Handwritten letters and cards

▶ Birth congratulations
▶ Engagement or wedding congratulations
▶ Condolences
▶ Special thanks
▶ Love letters

Typed communications

Formal letters such as letters of application are usually written on a computer, as they need to be very readable and clear. The same could be said of letters of complaint: if you are not satisfied with some goods or services you have purchased, your letter to the management must be precise, detailed and professional. Only then are you likely to receive a positive reply and some redress for your legitimate criticism.

Business letter writing is an important skill and need not be difficult, once you've mastered the basics covered in the next section of this chapter.

Again, you need to choose quality paper for printing if you want to look professional in your business dealings or to make an impact. Your choice of font or typeface in your word-processing package is equally important. There are many different kinds of fonts, some of which are easier to read than others. For professional letters, **Arial** and Times New Roman are standard choices. (Arial is slightly more modern and less ornate, while Times New Roman is slightly curlier and more serious looking.)

If typing a letter or email to a friend, you may wish to experiment with other typefaces for a more personal touch. Think about the recipient and what they might enjoy, as well as your own style of writing. The legibility of the font is important too – there's no point in carefully crafting a letter if your recipient can't easily read it.

Typed communication

▶ Business letters
▶ Letters to suppliers, such as your telephone or insurance company
▶ Explanatory letters
▶ Letters to the editor
▶ Job applications and CVs
▶ Emails – personal and professional

CHECKLIST

☐ Letter writing helps confirm the identities of both writer and recipient.

☐ Letters are *considered* communications, allowing reflection.

☐ Letters underline special occasions.

☐ Business communication is an important skill.

☐ It's important to choose the right kind of written communication for the occasion – handwritten or computer-generated letter, fax or email.

2

. . . .

From the Beginning to the End

This chapter discusses how to set out the elements that are essential to the beginning and end of every written communication. Formal invitations and replies are treated differently: see Chapter 3.

HOW TO BEGIN?

At the beginning, of course. For a typed or handwritten letter, that means at the top right-hand corner of your page. There you write the address from where you are writing the letter. This is usually home or the office, but can of course be where you are spending a holiday. An address should always be included. Remember, however, that you may need to use an address that is appropriate for a reply – a box number, for example.

Under the address comes the date. It should be set out as shown on the next page, all in the top right-hand corner.

Unit 5
137 Lyons Street
PRIDEVILLE
NSW 2716
18 July 2007

Why the date? Your letter may become part of social, family or company records, so it needs to include the date. Apart from that, it is interesting for the recipient of the letter to know when it was written. Sometimes the date is essential information, particularly if the letter involves making arrangements. So always put the date under your address in letters.

Dating emails and faxes is not important in the same way. Emails arrive ready-marked with the date and time of sending, as do most faxes. However, for formal faxes, such as to your insurance company regarding a claim, it is wise to also include the date under your address.

It is also often appropriate to include your telephone number in the information at the top of the letter. This goes opposite the first item of the address, next to the left-hand margin. If you are including a mobile phone number, fax number or email address, these go directly under the phone number. Don't forget to include the area code.

If it's a business letter, the name, title and business address of the person to whom you are writing come below the date, but on the left-hand side. The letter in Chapter 6 shows you how all this part of your business letter should look.

If sending an email, it is not necessary to include your address or phone number, as the recipient will automatically receive your email address with your message and can simply hit the 'Reply' button to respond. If you use email a lot for business correspondence, then investigate your email program's signature options. Most programs allow for a 'signature' to be included automatically at the end of each email, giving recipients details of your business address and contact numbers.

WHAT NEXT?

How you start any form of written communication is almost as important as what you say within the body of the text. Start badly, and you will lose your audience immediately. Misspelling your recipient's name or getting their title wrong are the most obvious pitfalls, so be sure to check how they like to be addressed.

Go to the left-hand margin of the page and on the next empty line write 'Dear So-and-so' or 'Sweetheart'. 'Dear Madam/Sir' should only be used for business letters. However, it's worth noting that you are far more likely to get a favourable response from the person you are contacting if you bother to ring and find out the name and title of the person with whom you are trying to do business.

Try to be imaginative in your form of address if you are writing a personal letter or email. It does make the whole experience more interesting for the recipient. If you've only been parted for a short time, 'Missing you already, Ivan, sweetheart,' is far more fun than 'Dear Ivan'. Let your imagination run riot, but always make your greeting to loved ones warm and welcoming.

NO PUNCTUATION?

Notice that it's not necessary to use end-of-line punctuation in the part of the letter you have written so far; layout and spacing does it all. The same applies to the greeting phrase that goes before your signature (e.g. 'Yours sincerely'). If, however, your letter ends with a whole sentence (e.g. 'I look forward to hearing from you soon.'), you should put a full stop after it in the usual way. The body of your message should be punctuated as normal.

THEN WHAT?

Try *not* to write, 'How are you?' or 'Hasn't the weather been wonderful?' (or cold or hot or whatever). They are clichés in letter writing. Think of the person to whom you are writing. Imagine the face of that person, or consider the occasion of the letter. Then think of something to say that has a direct relationship to your thoughts. You will then be able to write down something to create immediate rapport. It may be as simple as: 'The last time I saw you, you were wearing the scarf I gave you. Remember the day we chose it?' or 'Your company is such a family-oriented one that I feel sure you will be interested in this amusing family anecdote.'

It doesn't really matter what the subject is; what matters is the way you tackle it. A letter is a personal production, even if it is a business letter. It needs to sound like the writer, and you can accomplish this by being yourself, through your pen or keyboard. Indeed the greatest compliment you can pay a letter-writer is to say that reading the letter was like having a good conversation: the meaning is plain, and you have expressed yourself exactly as you would have in a two-way conversation. The most positive feeling any recipient of a letter can have comes from the personality implicit on the page.

Never dash off a few lines to any one, or to any business, without thinking a few moments about the person who will receive the letter; otherwise you may forget something crucial, or not do yourself justice.

There will be more information about this aspect of your letters later in this book, but let's leap forward to the conclusion of the letter. Here again the sky is the limit – almost.

▶ Decide what you are going to say before you begin.
▶ Ask yourself what the intention of the letter is.
▶ Check every paragraph to see if it achieves what you are trying to say.
▶ Read what you have written out loud so you can hear how it sounds.
▶ Decide whether it gets your meaning across and sounds natural.

CLOSING LINES

The time-honoured way to conclude a business letter is with the words 'Yours faithfully' or 'Yours truly'. If you begin the letter with 'Dear Madam/Sir', showing that you do not know the recipient by name, then you close the letter formally. If you have been able to write 'Dear Mrs O'Hara' or 'Dear Mr Janestzi' then you close with 'Yours sincerely'. If you are writing to a person you know, it may be more appropriate to conclude with 'All good wishes', or 'Warmest regards', or 'With my best wishes' – greetings that are businesslike but friendly. These endings are also more appropriate to business emails, which tend to be less formal in structure and style than letters.

When you are closing a letter to a friend or a member of your family, you have even greater freedom. You may use any blessing you choose: 'With all my love', 'Here's looking at you', 'Much love', 'Always', 'Bless you'. Any expression of feeling that pleases you at the time will undoubtedly give pleasure to the recipient of your thoughts.

SIGNING OFF

In a business letter, it is sensible to identify yourself in some way after your signature, as in the following example.

Caterina Belsarini
Administrative Officer

Or:

Joseph Burns
Sales Manager

If you want to make sure that your correspondent gets your title right, for example if your given name is a unisex one or you wish to be addressed as 'Miss' and not 'Ms', you should write the appropriate title in *brackets* before the name that follows your signature (see letters in Chapters 4, 5 and 6).

It is quite permissible to sign simply 'Caterina' or 'Joseph', with the identification below, if you know the people in the company well. This eliminates the sense of formality that might not sit well with the friendly tone of your letter.

In the case of family or friends, your first name is sufficient for your signature, but there is an exception to this: when you write a letter of condolence it is wise to put your surname in brackets after your signature. Many people may write to the grieving family. Over the passage of years, 'Bill' or 'Pat' is really not enough identification: the recipient may be left wondering 'Which Bill?' and it is upsetting not to be able to reply to such a letter.

It's also not a bad rule to follow for occasional correspondence if you have a name that is not distinctive. It's much the same as when the person on the other end of the phone says cheerily 'It's Ian!' (or Jill or Peter or Sue). You just happen to know five or six people of that name, and the voice in two words does not give you the clue you need.

If you have any doubts at all that the recipient of your letter will realise who is writing, put your surname as an afterthought. Of course it is helpful if you put your name and address on the back of the envelope but this is often forgotten or the envelope discarded. So do both.

The final piece of advice is this: sign your name legibly! We're all familiar with the scrawl at the end of a letter. Christmas cards seem to be the worst hazard: we scribble our way through scores of cards, and the writing becomes less and less clear as writer's cramp sets in. Try a little harder; make sure that those loving thoughts are known to have come from you! It's a matter of courtesy really – you should always put your correspondent in the position of being able to reply if he or she wishes to.

An example of what *not* to do is shown below. Without being able to decipher the signature, the recipient would have no way of contacting the writer easily.

Please don't hesitate to contact me if you require any further information.

Yours sincerely

Publicity Department

CHECKLIST

- Always include your address and the date.
- Avoid opening clichés.
- Treat your letter as a personal production.
- Make your signature legible.
- Identify yourself fully. If in doubt, include your surname.

3

Invitations

First let's think about formal invitations. They seem to cause more headaches than any other, despite the fact that they follow a formula and should therefore be easy.

KEEPING IT FORMAL

Formal invitations are usually sent for:

▶ a wedding reception
▶ an eighteenth or twenty-first birthday party
▶ a formal reception or opening
▶ a formal dance, ball or dinner.

Formal invitations should always be written in the third person, and shouldn't be signed. The 'third person' means 'Mr and Mrs Jonathan English', and not 'Jonathan and I'. The latter requires a signature, the former does not.

Following is an example of a formal wedding invitation. Purists will tell you that a wedding invitation should always be printed on a folded sheet of thick paper and that the measurements after folding ought to be five and a half inches by seven inches, with the smallest measurement at top and bottom. That idea is as outdated as the imperial system of measures it quotes. You may do what you like with the size and style of wedding invitations now, though remaining formal is still an appropriate choice since it is, after all, a solemn occasion and should be treated with some dignity.

Mr and Mrs Carl Schmidt

request the pleasure of your company

at the marriage of their daughter

Sara Elizabeth

to

Mr Ivan Cubella

at St James's Cathedral, Sydney

on Saturday 19 November 2007

at 5 p.m.

and afterwards at

The Grange, 55 Correa Street, North Sydney

RSVP 1 November   Black tie

Flat 4

231 Sturt Street

Paddington 2021

In this form you write the name of the person to receive the invitation in the top left-hand corner. One slight variation common for a formal invitation is to have the printer leave a space after the words 'the pleasure of the company of'; then you write the name of the invited person in the space. It is possibly easier to use the first option. It can be embarrassing to discover that there is not enough room for a dear friend whose name contains twenty letters – or more.

A contemporary version of the formal invitation acknowledges the equality of the sexes by making two small changes: the invitation begins 'Andrea and Carl Schmidt' and reads 'Sara Elizabeth and Ivan Cubella'. Both generations may prefer this form.

The traditional invitation assumes that the bride's parents (or others of the parents' generation) are acting as hosts, and the invitation is sent out in their names. Where parents of the bride are divorced it can be a little tricky. If there is no animosity between the parents, they may well combine for this occasion, wishing to make their daughter's wedding as happy as possible. The wording should then be 'Mr Nicholas Braithwaite and Mrs Georgina Braithwaite request the pleasure of your company'. In each case, the order of the names may be reversed. If the mother has reverted to her maiden name after divorce, this should be used instead.

If the father or mother of the bride has been widowed, the invitation goes out in the one name: 'Mr Rodney Collins (or Mrs Cecilia Shaw) requests the pleasure of your company'. If a widow or widower has remarried, the names of the parent and partner appear as host and hostess. Where the mother of the bride now has a different surname from her daughter, it is wise to include the bride's surname on the invitation to avoid any confusion or embarrassment.

Where couples are marrying for the second time or are older, much depends on the style of the reception. Most often the couple issues the invitation in their own names: 'Ms Anita Brookman and Mr Claudio Minotti request the pleasure of your company'; and often these invitations are more informal than those for younger people, or for a first wedding.

If you are having the invitations printed, the printer will be able to advise you about details of layout, whatever style you have chosen.

FORMAL REPLIES

Formal invitations to weddings, balls, parties or receptions should be answered formally, again in the third person. It is, in fact, a repeat of the essential wording of the invitation. Here is an example of an answer received to the Schmidt wedding. It should be handwritten on good-quality unlined writing paper or on a card and set out as a paragraph. You may begin with 'Mary and Alan McDonald' instead of 'Dr and Mrs Alan McDonald' if you wish.

Dr and Mrs Alan McDonald thank Mr and Mrs Schmidt for their kind invitation to the wedding of their daughter Sara Elizabeth to Mr Ivan Cubella at St James's Cathedral, Sydney on Saturday 19 November at 5 p.m. and afterwards at the Grange, North Sydney, and have much pleasure in accepting.

If you are unable to attend because of a commitment already made, you begin the same way but conclude with '… The Grange, North Sydney, but regret that they are unable to accept because of a previous engagement'. If your reason is illness or distance (or no desire to see your ex get married, you may conclude with '…unable to attend' or a brief indication of your reason. A separate informal note to explain in more detail can then be sent with the formal reply.

You may, if you wish, omit the place of the reception from your reply. Because you will be attending the wedding, it is implicit that you will be at the reception also, so a shorter version is quite acceptable.

The same formula is applied to formal invitations for other functions. Simply reiterate the wording of the invitation and either accept or express your regret, stating your reason courteously. Remember that replies to weddings, in particular, are often kept for years; yours may become part of history.

AN INFORMAL NOTE

Informal invitations can take any form these days, so long as they are clear about the place and time of the event. Designing your own invitations is great fun, and to receive an individual card reflecting the characters of the hosts gives a boost to the function even before it has begun.

Of course you do not have to do this. You might prefer just to write something simple, such as the following two examples (put your address and date at the top, as described in Chapter 2).

Dear Matthew and Terry

We are having a party on Friday 13 March designed to scare you witless. Do come and join us, in costume. You might even spook the superstitions. We plan to ring the graveyard bell at 9 p.m. We look forward to your ghoulish appearance then.

With love
Lynne and Tinor

• • •

Please, Maddy and Ken

Come to our drinks party on Saturday December 11 any time from 6.30 to 8.30 p.m. We look forward to seeing you then.

Cheers
Yvonne and Andrew

With most people having access to email nowadays, invitations may be sent this way too – either as a simple note in the body text or as an attached document.

INFORMAL REPLIES

In informal invitations, the phone number or email address is often included at the top for an easy reply. If you are writing an informal reply, write your address, date and contact details at the top, then take your cue from the tenor of the invitation. Here are two examples.

Dear Lynne and Tinor
We shall be happy to appear at your ghostly evening on March 13, from 9 o'clock by the bell. We look forward to frightening you and the other guests.

Yours eerily
Terry and Matthew

* * *

Of course, dear Yvonne and Andrew
We shall be with you for drinks on December 11 between 6.30 and 8.30. What a good way to welcome in the festive season.

Happily
Maddy and Ken

It is even acceptable simply to write with a flourishing hand, 'We are coming!' and then sign your names. The exclamation mark in this case says it all: 'Wow, what a good idea; try to stop us!'

So with informality, it is all to do with successful communication, and keeping those lines open makes for many a joyous event.

If you have to decline an informal invitation, make your reply, like the two examples that follow, as regretful as possible; a warm personal note softens the blow.

Dear Lynne and Tinor

I am so sorry that I can't be with you to scare everyone on Friday 13 March. I shall be in Amsterdam then – fun, I know, but I wish I could be in two places at the same time. Hope it's a great, scary success.

Love
Stephanie

•   •   •

My dears

I cannot be with you on December 11 for I will be in Prince Henry's Hospital for a small operation on my foot. Just wish I could be with you. I will hobble in before Christmas to hear all about the party, and to share my operation with you.

Sorrowfully
Mario

RSVP

This is a shortened form of *Répondez, s'il vous plait* ('Please reply'). Now there seems to have grown up an idea that if RSVP if printed on the bottom of any invitation, with a date, that is the date on which you are expected to reply. This is not so: the date means this is the *last* day on which your host and hostess expect to receive your answer.

Knowing the numbers early is all-important for catering, so reply as soon as you possibly can after the invitation has arrived. Your hosts will appreciate your consideration – and your obvious commitment. People often put off replying until the last minute. Are they hoping for something better to turn up? If they are, they don't deserve to be included on any guest list – let alone yours!

TIMING THE INVITATION

Is there any hard and fast rule about when an invitation for a function should be issued? No, there isn't, though a rule of thumb would be the earlier the better, especially for big occasions. There is a great deal to do to organise a wedding, for example, and the sooner the host and hostess know the numbers of people who are able to come, the easier the planning will be. In addition, those invited are more likely to be free on the day. In this case invitations should *arrive* at least six weeks before the set date.

For an occasion that is important but not world shattering, three weeks is plenty of notice: sending an invitation on the fourth of one month for an event on the fourth of the next is fine.

Of course, there is the last minute idea, which often works beautifully. A phone call suggesting a get-together for the following night, or the coming weekend, can be the start of a most enjoyable time. The advantage is that you will know instantly whether your invitation is accepted or not. But for a function requiring a lot of planning, written replies are more useful: planning notes ('should sit next to the Smiths' or 'vegetarian') may be made on them for other organisers to refer to; and they are reliable documents for getting place cards right, for memorising guests' names, or for choosing speakers.

For the person invited it all comes down to consideration for others. The people asking you to attend have gone to some trouble to make sure that you've been asked and that you know all the details of the coming function. All you have to do is reply promptly, honour your commitment and enjoy yourself!

CHECKLIST

- Write formal invitations in the third person.
- Formal invitations need a formal reply.
- Informal invitations may have a casual reply.
- If you cannot accept, always give a courteous reason for declining.
- Answer any invitation as soon as you can.

4

Special Letters

Each type of letter discussed in this chapter is based on a simple formula. Once you understand the formula, the letter is much easier to write: you simply adapt it to fit the particular circumstances.

THANKS

Thank-you letters can vary greatly. They will be as different as the occasions that have prompted the thank-you note. They do have elements in common, however: they should express appreciation, mention something specific, and be handwritten wherever possible. One exception to this is for business services rendered, in which case a typed letter or email may suffice.

Imagine that you have been a guest during a trip away from home. Your room was thoughtfully prepared with flowers and books, you were well fed, and invited to use the phone and internet for planning ahead. The next morning you were entertained with a long walk on the beach and a swim with the family before a barbecue lunch to which some delightful local people had been invited and then you'd been driven to the nearest railway station, twenty kilometres away, to catch your train. After that – silence.

Why didn't you write immediately to tell your hosts what a good weekend it had been? You didn't have time? You meant to, but the right words didn't come?

Not good enough: a great deal of time and trouble had been expended to give you a relaxing, thoroughly enjoyable break. Don't miss the opportunity to cement good relationships by writing your prompt thanks. Something like the following will do.

Tel: (07) 987 6543

41 Palm Tree Close
Northern Beach
QLD 4321

20 March 2006

Dear Julie and Chris

I very much enjoyed my time with you. Everything you did for my pleasure and my comfort was appreciated, and I particularly enjoyed meeting the Mercurios and McBains. Thank you both for going to so much trouble for me: it was great to have such a delightful break and a bit of family life again. I look forward to seeing you both when visit my part of the world in September.

With my warmest thanks

Jamie Lim

The right words are easy to find: all you do is remember what you considered the highlights of the visit and mention them. It does not need to be a long letter (though it may be if you wish), but it *does* need to be sincere. Your hosts then know that the pleasure felt has been prolonged, and that the preparation was well worth it. The Latin aphorism *Bis dat qui cito dat* ('He gives twice who gives quickly') is certainly apt here. Your early letter of thanks means you were still thinking of the occasion when you wrote, and that thought lets your hosts know that the visit was a success.

Thank-you notes can be sent after a dinner party too, especially if it has been a formal one with carefully chosen guests and an elaborate menu. An appreciative email may be more appropriate for an impromptu dinner with friends.

Upon receiving a gift a letter of thanks is also required. The habit of ignoring gifts is to be deplored. When parcels are sent seemingly into the wide blue yonder – since no acknowledgement is ever made – the sender never knows if the gift has arrived, given pleasure, been useful, or if receiving it ever gave the recipient the lift that was intended.

Thank-you letters are really two-way things: they acknowledge the giver's generosity, and they give further pleasure to the giver when received. When writing one, the trick is to mention some aspect of the gift that is most appreciated. This tells the giver that the gift has arrived in good order, that it will be found useful, and that the style was liked by the recipient: 'I will take your book away with me next weekend, and I'm looking forward to reading it'; 'Your flowers filled the house with colour and perfume'; 'Your congratulatory card has pride of place in my room and I am enjoying its sentiments as I write to you'; or 'Joshua needed more booties as the temperature dropped, so your gift could not have been more timely'. The variations are limitless. Giving pleasure for pleasure received is not difficult.

Remember that the more specific you can be, the better the communication. The bald note that says, 'Thank you for our wedding gift' really says nothing at all. The following short note says much more.

Dear Harrison

The gift you sent us for our wedding was wonderful. The cups and saucers matched our coffee set exactly, and will be in constant use. We do appreciate the fact that you took the trouble to choose something you knew would give us pleasure. Thank you for your beautiful and thoughtful gift.

Our best wishes and thanks

Miriam and Enzo

The mention of the design of the cups and the assurance that they will be in constant use tell the giver that the gift has been noticed, and that it was something the couple really wanted. It's a much more satisfying letter to receive than the first example, which was certainly not specific.

CONDOLENCES

For some reason many people find letters of sympathy the most difficult to write. Yet they bring such comfort at a time of bereavement that we should all strive to write them well. A card with a printed verse or sentiment, while comforting, is not the same because it cannot convey the personal loss you feel or your appreciation of the person who has died.

Letters of condolence do not need to be long. They should express exactly what you want them to, and they should show sympathy with the bereaved. Even if you do not know the person well there will be something you can share. Here are some examples to help you.

Dear Mrs Peck

I am writing to express my sympathy on the loss of your husband. We worked together at Visions Splendid all those years ago, and he had a special place in my heart. It was Mr Peck who welcomed me to the company and who kept a fatherly eye on my progress. He always had a smile for me, a kindly word, and a willingness to help me solve any problems. I wanted you to know that I shall never forget his kindness.

He was a generally loved and respected figure in the company, and I am sure many others share my recollections of him. May our thoughts comfort you at this sad time.

Most sincerely

Anna Polansky

Dear Alessandra and Louis

We were shocked to learn of Lee-Anne's death, and we feel helpless in the face of this tragic loss. Her bright little face, her curiosity and her mischievous air will always be remembered with much fondness in our family. We will never forget your little daughter, and all our thoughts are with you at this sad time.

With our loving sympathy

Gina and Steve

Or:

Dear Joe

I was saddened to hear of your mother's death. When we were all at school she always made me welcome at your home, with a cheerful word and lots of food. She had the rare gift of creating warmth about her, and that's what I shall remember best.

My thoughts are with you and all the family.

With sincere sympathy

Hamish McGregor

Your message of condolence need not be a traditional letter. It can be a poem you can share, the words of a song, or a prayer. Here is a prayer I wrote for a young friend when her husband suddenly died and she was left to bring up two very small children.

Dear Lord give me understanding,
    for the Lord knows I need it at this time.
Dear Lord help me to overcome my despair,
    for the Lord knows I am suffering from it now.
Dear Lord grant me inner peace
    for the Lord knows I am in turmoil within,
Dear Lord allow me to express my grief,
    for the Lord knows I need to do this.
Dear Lord heal my wounds,
    for the Lord knows I bleed silently within.
Dear Lord overcome my anger at my fate,
    for the Lord knows I want to cry 'Why me? Why me?'
Dear Lord show me the way to fill this aching void
    for the Lord knows how deep it really is.
Dear Lord thank you for the support of my family,
    for the Lord knows I cherish their comfort.
Dear Lord promise me your strength,
    for the Lord knows that He alone can bring me and my children through this crisis.
That is my strength.

Whatever you decide to write in such circumstances you should always do it at once. A letter sent immediately is especially appreciated because it is a clear demonstration of your concern for the bereaved.

When you sit down to write your letter of condolence, concentrate especially on recalling the person who has died: remember characteristics, remind yourself of past times, call up happy memories, and the letter will be easier to write. It will also convey understanding and sympathy, and its sincerity will be plain.

It was once unheard of, but is now quite acceptable, to include a postscript to your letter: 'I shall quite understand if you do not reply to this letter for you will have many to acknowledge'. This has its hazards, however. To know that the loss has been shared is a comfort to the writer, too; not to hear back leaves another sense of loss. Moreover, replying may be an important part of the grieving process for the recipient. In any case, *always* include your address on a letter of condolence so that the recipient can easily reply.

Most often, the bereaved family formulates a short paragraph that can be printed on a plain white card, to use as an acknowledgement of the majority of the letters. A personal message can be added to the card if this is thought suitable. The wording on the card is usually something like this.

The family of the late Benjamin David Joseph
acknowledges with grateful thanks
the kind thoughts, deeds and expressions of sympathy
upon the loss of their dearly loved husband, father and grandfather.

26.10.1935 – 2.11.2006

When the person who has died has been a public figure and hundreds of letters and cards have been received, it is difficult for one member of the family to reply to them all. In this instance other family members need to help. There is really no substitute for individual replies, even if the task takes some weeks.

CONGRATULATIONS

What a happy task this is, to be able to write your congratulations to someone you know. The pleasure you feel comes through your words, and so gives pleasure to the recipient.

Think of the event you are celebrating: think of how happy you are for the person; and presto! out pops your letter. An engagement, a graduation, a sporting first, a promotion, the birth of a child, an anniversary or birthday, a leap from primary to secondary school – anything that is worthy of celebration is worthy of a congratulatory letter. 'We were delighted to hear …' is a standard beginning for this type of letter. After that opening you might comment on the particular situation and conclude with your best wishes. Or you can be less formal.

For congratulations on a good exam result, you might start your letter with: 'Well done, Michael' or 'How wonderful, Michelle!' For an anniversary, how about: 'Fifty years, Mum and Dad? I can't believe it!' An eighteenth or twenty-first birthday might bring out 'Congratulations, dear Bruno! We can remember …' A new appointment could see you in a whimsical mood: 'Dear Councillor Reagan (isn't it great to be able to write that?)'. A sporting victory could well begin with 'Dear Captain for the Premier side, We are all thrilled to bits with your win'.

If you are not comfortable with these informal openings, or if you can't think of anything original, fall back on a more traditional formula.

Dear Tracey and Jack

The news of your approaching wedding has given us great joy. We do hope that your future will be filled with happiness, and that the wedding day itself will be filled with sunshine. We remember many happy times with your families when we were all younger, and know that this union will be blessed.

With congratulations and our love
Alistair and Elizabeth

Or for a grandchild:

Dear Yasmin

We can't believe that you are old enough to leave sixth grade and go to high school next year. You really are growing up. You will find it very different, but very interesting. We will think of you next Tuesday, and wish you the best day possible.

Our congratulations and lots of love
Grandma and Grandpa

Whichever format you decide to follow, *do it*. There is nothing like receiving a letter to bring pleasure, and usually the more unexpected it is the greater the delight. So send your congratulations around the world! For a major milestone in life, a handwritten letter is better than an email, as the recipient may like to look back on it in years to come.

ENCOURAGEMENT

If you know someone is working particularly hard to achieve something, then a warm letter to encourage an even greater effort would be very welcome. They don't have to be elaborate or long letters, indeed the shorter the better. Even a quick email will suffice. All you need to do is make sure your words show that you understand the hard work being done, and that your thoughts are with the person undertaking the task.

Dear Auntie Louise

This letter is to wish my eldest aunt good luck. I'm just dazzled by the progress you have made with your PhD. I've always thought your subject sounded interesting and now Dad tells me that you're almost ready to write up your thesis.

Yours will be a hard act to follow.

Your affectionate nephew
Dermot

Jed, my old mate

I heard today of the rehabilitation program you've undertaken since the accident. It sounds like a helluva job, but if anyone can stick to it and get back to full health, it's you.

My best wishes as always
Paul

Again, just let your mind roam free about the person to whom your words are being addressed. Then it won't be difficult to say exactly what you mean.

COMPLAINTS

Letters of complaint cover an enormous field, from barking dogs to loud music to faulty products and neighbourhood rows.

In each instance a letter of complaint should be written very carefully indeed. After all, you don't want to trigger off legal action because you did not word your letter accurately. Let's begin with a simple note about dissatisfaction with a product you bought at a supermarket.

Look for the name of the manufacturer and the address listed on the packet. When you have determined this, write to the Sales Manager or the Marketing Manager as follows. Include your address and the date in the top right-hand corner. Then precede the salutation with the title of the person to whom you are writing and the address of the company, as shown below.

You will notice that the letter states the date of purchase; the company and the place from which the purchase was made; the reasons for the complaint; and the action the writer would like to see taken.

Tel: (08) 321 4321

33 Eucalypt Road
WOODLAND PARK
SA 5432

20 January 2007

The Sales Manager
Wispy Standards Ltd
PO Box 147
COMPTON
NSW 2159

Dear Sir/Madam

On 18 January 2007 I purchased from Safeway in Woodland Park, SA, a packet of Wisps, manufactured by your company. The packet information stated that the Wisps were salted and garlic-flavoured. They were neither. The flavour appears to be orange; please check the packet, which I enclose.

Would you please explain what has happened, and supply me with a replacement packet of salted, garlic-flavoured Wisps?

I look forward to your early reply

Yours faithfully

P. Minopoulos

(Ms) Phillipa Minopolous

The letter has not been written in an aggressive tone, but it does assert the rights of the shopper to buy a product that matches advertising claims, and it does show that you expect a prompt, positive response.

The answer to such a letter will probably be that the batch was wrongly packaged, and you will certainly receive your packet of Wisps very soon after your letter reaches the desk of the Sales Manager. No company wants dissatisfied customers, for the damage to their public relations campaign can be considerable. If more consumers were to complain in a constructive and informative way, the products on our supermarket shelves might be greatly improved.

The letter saying YOUR PRODUCT IS LOUSY may not even elicit a reply. Nor does it deserve one; the tone of your letter should be formal and courteous.

It is wise to return the faulty product to the manufacturer to prove your point, though this may not always be possible. It is helpful to the company if an analysis needs to be made, and the result may be an improvement – all because you took the time and trouble to complain in a positive manner.

It is the tone of the letter that is important – and the facts are essential. Of course, you may be complaining about a service that was rendered poorly or not at all. In that case you must be clear about the time and the circumstances, and you must name or describe the person or persons at fault. You must explain what happened or did not happen, and your reasons for being upset by this lack of service. Redress isn't always practicable, but your complaint may at least ensure that the same thing will not happen to others.

Neighbourhood rows really ought to be settled face to face if at all possible, but when this has failed a letter is the next resort. Don't rush from a verbal exchange to litigation. A personal, carefully worded letter will show that you are serious about your complaint but it will also leave doors open well short of the courtroom and those attendant expenses.

Try the 'softly-softly' approach, but be explicit, and definite about what you expect. The next letter is an example of the approach you might like to take.

25 Happiness Drive
PARADISE 3210

16 January 2007

Mr Norm Neighbour
23 Happiness Drive
PARADISE 3210

Dear Norm

We have spoken about the loud music coming from your son's sleepout on numerous occasions. So far nothing has happened to remedy the situation. We are being driven mad by it, especially after 11.30 at night. We both need our sleep because our workloads are heavy, but the constant beat keeps us awake into the small hours. Would you see that Hugo keeps the volume down, please?

If he does not comply we shall have to report the problem to the appropriate authorities. In view of our good relationship over the years, we have no wish to do this, but if there is not an immediate improvement we are left with no alternative.

Yours sincerely

Serena and Tim Noyes

The type of letter given in the previous example may be adapted to suit any circumstances that are troublesome between neighbours.

Most people prefer friendly relationships in the area where they live, so it is best to keep your letter as low-key as possible. You are entitled to your peace and quiet, so you are well within your rights to complain, but do it carefully, hoping to retain that good atmosphere you now enjoy. After all, you don't want to set up a vendetta, the result of which might see you selling up and moving away from the neighbourhood you now like (apart from barking dogs, loud noise, pollution, misuse of parkland, screaming children, and so on).

If you need to write a letter complaining about an account you have received for work done, you really must be explicit, particularly if you think you have been overcharged.

When you have had a written quote for the work that was to be undertaken it is easy to prove your point, especially if you have taken the trouble to write and accept the quote before the work begins. However, if this is not the case, do not be deterred: take the time to make a list for yourself of the shortcomings in the finished task, and then write your letter, clearly listing the deficiencies, as shown in the following letter.

Tel: 511 8795

5 Challenge Close
NEW VENTURE
VIC 3131

7 April 2007

Mr Patrick Head
Pavers To Dance On
34 Acacia Road
WOODS RETREAT
VIC 3133

Dear Mr Head

I wish to draw your attention to the account I received from you for work done at my house in the period 3–14 March 2007.

You appear not to have received the cheque made out to you and given to your workers on 14 March. That cheque was for three-quarters of the quoted amount and represented payment for the work satisfactorily completed to date. I withheld the remainder because parts of the total job were unsatisfactory. Details are as follows:

1. Your quote included the levelling and paving of the area to the south of the front veranda. This area has been levelled but not paved.

2. As detailed in your quote, the extension of the back patio paving was to be the same width as the existing paving but, at present, it is narrower by two rows of bricks.

3. The concrete gutter listed in your quote has not been constructed.

I discussed these matters with your workers and they assured me that they would return in a week to complete the job. This has not happened, nor have repeated messages on your answering machine brought any response.

I request that the work be satisfactorily completed without delay, and I shall then be happy to pay the remainder of the amount. I refer you to the enclosed copies of your quote and my acceptance.

Yours sincerely

Kerry O'Reilly

(Mr) Kerry O'Reilly

Again, there is nothing aggressive about the letter. The date of the work has been given and the details of your complaint have been set out succinctly, so that the manager of the business should be able to assess the situation quickly and act accordingly.

With such letters there are some guidelines.

▶ Always state your case as simply as possible.
▶ List the problems as you see them.
▶ Offer a solution if possible.
▶ Convey your expectation that the matter will be resolved to your satisfaction.

▶ Include the date and place of your purchase or of the event.
▶ Refer to your records, for example a written quote and your written acceptance.

CHECKLIST

Always write a thank-you letter or email within a few days.

Personal letters after a bereavement are better than printed cards.

Letters of congratulation need to be cheery, and are better short than long.

Letters of complaint should be specific but not aggressive.

5

Job Applications

Letters of application are so important that they deserve a chapter to themselves. Your future may depend on the way you answer a job advertisement, so it is crucial that you make the best possible impression when you write. And for employers, the tactful, encouraging letter to the unsuccessful applicant should be part of the organisation's good image.

THE APPLICANT'S LETTER

You need to design your application so that your prospective employer will want to interview you. Remember that your job application may be one of many; therefore it must look good and read well.

If an application arrives on a scrappy piece of paper, ill written and ill spelt, it will not be regarded seriously. 'I am applying for the job advertised in Saturdays newspaper. Joe Bloggs' – will not get Joe anywhere. Sometimes the Joe Bloggses of this world even forget to include an address or phone number. That is essential information, and if it is forgotten there is certainly no hope of an interview.

So what do you do to help yourself?

Read the advertisement carefully, and answer it in the way it instructs you. If it says applications should be emailed, do that. If it asks for your handwriting, write the application out legibly on good, plain, unlined writing paper, using a line guide underneath the page. (Some companies do this so they can analyse your handwriting, but you would still generally send a typed CV). If it states that you need to include a certain reference number, make sure you do. If the advertisement asks for the names of three referees, give them. If it clearly states that experience is needed, say where you have worked previously. If the applications close on the last day of April, make certain that your letter arrives before that date.

In other words, follow the 'rules' as set out in the job advertisement. Neglecting to do so will only irritate those receiving the applications, as there will be gaps in the knowledge they need when making a short list.

Ask an experienced person to read your application when you have written it. Be prepared to re-draft until you are confident that you are putting your best letter forward. Use the following as a guide.

A good application

Tel: (03) 753 6601 (A.H.)

17 The Parade
CLIFTON GRANGE
VIC 3299

18 April 2007

Ms Trish Margettis
The Human Resources Manager
Boxed Containers Ltd
45–49 Badenoch Street
ADELAIDE 5000

Dear Ms Margettis

I wish to apply for the position advertised in *The Australian*, Saturday 17 April 2007 (your reference number 703/A).

I believe that I have the skills you are looking for in an office manager. My experience includes two years with ABC Radio Australia; three years with Scotch College, Melbourne; and five years with my current employer, Computers Victoria Ltd. In the last two positions I have been office manager, and have enjoyed the responsibility.

As well as having administrative skills, I type at the rate of 66 words per minute, am computer literate and have familiarity with Microsoft Word, PowerPoint, Excel and a range of other programs.

I was born in Adelaide and have wanted to return there to work for a long time. Your company is known to me, and I understand your expansion into the overseas market is imminent. As I am fluent in Indonesian I am hoping that you might be able to use this skill to the company's advantage.

The three referees' names you asked for are on a separate sheet, attached to this letter of application. My curriculum vitae is also enclosed.

I look forward to hearing from you and hope that an interview will follow this application.

Yours sincerely

Janet Home

(Ms) Janet Home

Let's examine what Janet Home did that was correct.

She has given her address and telephone number and has made sure that she has correctly given the name, title and address of the advertiser. As the HR manager's name was mentioned in the advertisement she has used it in her letter. As requested, she has quoted the reference number. She has given details of her experience and has added the extra skills she believes may be important in this position. She explains her interest in working in Adelaide, and shows some knowledge of the company. She has taken the opportunity to mention her knowledge of Indonesian; that may be her trump card.

Applicants were asked to name three referees and this Janet has done. (You should always ask a referee's permission to use his or her name before including it on your application.) She has included her CV. Janet has written fluently, her spelling is correct, and her letter is appropriately paragraphed. She has concluded on a hopeful note, and has signed her letter legibly, with the typewritten follow-up just in case.

Let's look at the other side of the coin. What might Janet have done that could mean she would not hear from the company? Her reply might have looked something like the following letter.

A poor application

17 The Parade
CLIFTON GRANGE

The HR Manager
Boxed Containers Ltd
ADELAIDE SA

Dear Trish
I wish to apply for the position advertised in *The Australian*.

I think I have the skills you are looking for, as I have been in a similar position for the past five years.

I type well and understand computers.

I was born in Adelaide and know your company well. My knowledge of Indonesian might be useful to you. I can bring my referees' names when I come for an interview.

Yours sincerely

[signature]

So what did Janet do wrong?

First she forgot to date her application, and referred merely to a position advertised in *The Australian*. Which advertisement? Such a large company as Boxed Containers Ltd (whose address Janet leaves incomplete) would be looking for staff in all departments at most times. So what position was Janet seeking? Even when she came to selling her qualifications, she did not go into details but simply said she had held a similar position for five years. What type of position? Where? The only clue about which job she might be looking for comes with her statement that she types well and is comfortable with computers.

She tells the HR manager that she was born in Adelaide, but makes no mention of wishing to return. She has apparently done no research into the company's current image, and is therefore not in a position to mention their plans for overseas marketing, where her Indonesian might be of benefit to them.

Though asked to included referees' names with the application, Janet assumes that she will be granted an interview and that it is permissible to bring those names then. She makes no mention of her CV. Her paragraphing is awkward: more detail would have helped that problem. Her signature is hard to read and there is no typed name beneath it, so it becomes increasingly difficult to answer this application at all.

Janet does not quote the reference number that was published in the advertisement, and she addressed the HR manager by her first name. This is customary in many situations, but is certainly not acceptable when writing a letter of application.

So this time round, Janet Home will not be receiving a positive reply from Boxed Containers. And who could blame them?

Writing a job application is not entering a competition, but at times it may feel like that. The letter is your first hurdle, a means of obtaining an interview, so it must reflect you and your capabilities. Include everything you think would put your name on the short list for that particular job, but try not to be too fulsome about yourself. It's a fine line, but one you must tread if you are to succeed.

Take the time and effort to prepare a really good letter and CV. Then you will probably find that you need make only minor changes for subsequent job applications.

YOUR CURRICULUM VITAE

What exactly is the curriculum vitae you might need to supply with your job application? The Latin means 'course of life', and the Concise Oxford defines it as a 'brief account of one's previous career'. Most CVs are more detailed than that, for they usually begin with education (from secondary level to higher education, then listing any degrees, diplomas or postgraduate qualifications achieved). Next comes the list of positions held from leaving school, university or college to the present day.

Personal details (age, marital status, number of children, for example) are optional, but age or birth date is usually included. For older applicants with a long working career it is sometimes sufficient to list in some detail the last three positions held, including responsibilities, position in the company, achievements, and so forth. Applicants for senior positions often list career events in *reverse* order, giving priority and most detail to the most recent positions held.

Sometimes it is appropriate to have two versions of your CV: a brief version, which you send with your application, and a longer version that you offer to send if required.

Your CV is an entirely separate document from any letter of application you may write. You should file your CV and update it as required. It should look *good*: set it out attractively on good, plain paper and use a folder if it is long.

THE EMPLOYER'S RESPONSE

When as an employer you have advertised a position it is up to you to reply to each one (given that you can read the signature and that the address has been supplied). A blunt 'Your application was unsuccessful' is not good enough.

So how do you word such a reply? It is best to be kind and truthful and in most cases it *is* possible to be both. How about the following examples?

Dear Ms Home

Thank you for your application for the position of office manager recently advertised by Boxed Containers Ltd.

We received a surprisingly large number of replies, and it was difficult to make a choice from the many applicants. We regret to inform you that you were not successful on this occasion. However, we are keeping your application on file in case a position arises for which your qualifications are appropriate.

With every good wish

Yours truly

Trish Margettis

Trish Margettis
Human Resources Manager

Dear Ms Home

Thank you for your recent application for the position of office manager at Boxed Containers Ltd, and for your interest in the company. We considered your application carefully but regret to inform you that on this occasion you have not been successful.

We wish you success with your future job applications.

Yours truly

Trish Margettis

Trish Margettis
Human Resources Manager

CHECKLIST

A letter of application should be as perfect as possible.

Do exactly what the advertisement instructs you to do.

Set your application out clearly and check your spelling.

Sign your name legibly.

If you are an employer, all letters of application should be answered.

6

. . . .

Business Letters

This is a broad topic, since any letter that 'works for you' can be described as a business letter. Whether the communication is a one-to-one thing or between you and an organisation, the essence of the letter remains the same: some action is needed. Your business letters will often follow preliminary telephone enquiries about the person to whom you should write, whether that company makes the goods you need, if any accommodation is available, and so on. Nowadays, many less-formal business matters can be dealt with via email. However, the same basic principles apply.

Business letters should always be easily read and understood. The paragraphs of a business letter should not be indented; instead, leave one line between paragraphs to make it clearer to read. If writing a letter of more than one page, always number the pages; for example, Page 1/3, so that if pages become lost or separated, everything will be a lot clearer to your recipient.

Paint Solutions
Orana House
7 Coventry Street
Hawthorn 3219

Peter Moore
Chief Buyer
Apricot Housing
Nunawading Industrial Estate
Nunawading 3133

21 January 2007

Dear Peter

Re: Revised Quote No. 389659 (paints)

Thank you for your letter requesting further quotes for the paint.

We can now supply concrete paints in a number of different colours, as per the enclosed samples, so please specify colour when you send us your final spec prior to us providing the above revised quotation.

I look forward to hearing from you again soon.

Yours sincerely

Anna Truss
Managing Director

ORGANISING A HOLIDAY

Your letter seeking accommodation at a holiday hotel is one kind of business letter. Set out the details so that the proprietor knows exactly what your needs are.

▶ Dates – day of arrival, day of departure
▶ Number of people – adults and children
▶ If there is a baby, is a cot needed?
▶ Deposit enclosed, if required
▶ Any special needs – dietary, or a front room or a quiet room, or a double or two single beds for a couple

Of course your postal address will head the letter. Make sure you add your phone number (and maybe your email or fax details) so that the confirmation can be made quickly and easily. Work addresses and telephone numbers may be appropriate in this instance.

PLACING AN ORDER

In writing to a company to place an order, use the same technique. Mention the article you wish to buy, give details about it so there can be no mistake, mention that you have included payment with the order or arranged for an internet transfer, confirm the method of delivery if appropriate, and thank them for their attention.

The trick is to be concise and accurate. Get the 'business' over in a business-like manner, and the results will be much better.

CHANGING YOUR ADDRESS

If you have moved from one address to another, you should notify all the companies with whom you have dealings. This can be done very simply.

On a plain piece of paper, write your former address, and the names that have been used in that account. Under that, re-state the names you wish to remain registered, mentioning any alterations. Follow this with the new address. If there is a new phone number, fax or email address, this should be on a separate line for clarity and ease of access.

If you are attending to this before the date of the move, make certain that you state clearly the date from which this new information is valid. Emailing this information to regular correspondents could also prove useful.

SEEKING INFORMATION

There are times when you need to have more information about something. You write for this extra information in the same businesslike manner. Let's imagine that you want to know a good deal more about a particular rose you have seen advertised, available only interstate. Make a list of the gaps in your knowledge, then put the questions into an efficient framework and construct your letter or email.

Tel: (02) 487 3217
Fax: (02) 589 4187

PO Box 189B
TORQUAY
VIC 3228

28 September 2006

The Manager
Aldgate Roses
5–9 Secrecy Road
ALDGATE
SA 5054

Dear Sir/Madam

I read with interest your advertisement for old world roses in last month's Garden Guide. Would you please give me some more details about the Iceland Poppy Rose?

1. Will it grow in sandy soil near the beach?
2. Is it delicately or strongly perfumed?
3. Does it have large thorns as so many old roses do?
4. What colour is it?
5. Is it a long-living rose?
6. Will it endure a certain amount of neglect or must it be nurtured?
7. Would the Iceland Poppy Rose also be suited to conditions in the Dandenong Ranges outside Melbourne?
8. Would you be willing to offer me a discount price for an order of a dozen bushes?

I look forward to your reply.

Yours truly

LRGardiner

(Mrs) Rose Gardiner

Mrs Gardiner has listed the questions in point form. This makes it very easy for the owner of the nursery to list the replies just as concisely. A rambling letter with long sentences means that the owner has to wade through the language to get to the crux of the matter. This is time-consuming, and in the long run may not be very productive for the questioner.

You may use point form in any letter seeking advice or information. Or you can use 'bullets' – see the lists in the boxes at the end of the chapters as an example. Businesses are usually short of time, and the easier the letter-writer makes it the more likely a prompt reply is – and that's what you're aiming for.

CHECKLIST

- A business letter needs to be simple and specific.
- Include your address, telephone and fax numbers, and email address.
- Make sure your letter covers all the points you want to know about.
- Write in point from if you want a straightforward answer quickly.

7

Faxes

Faxes are an important part of business communication; they may also be used for personal communication, although email is generally faster and more convenient.

As a means of communication, fax is far speedier than post and has the great advantage of leaving the sender with the original as a record. And unlike email, a fax can be hand written or drawn. It's ideal for quickly sending forms that must be filled in by hand. The fax has many benefits, but there are some points worth remembering.

THE FAX FOR BUSINESS LETTERS

Your letter has been written and has been faxed within a few moments of its completion. There has been no chance to have second thoughts, as there is if the letter has to be copied or printed or if it waits for the post. When your letter emerges from the fax, you see that it is missing a vital fact or – much worse – could be misinterpreted.

It's a good rule to be very sure of your letter before you fax it off, even if this means a little delay. Always be confident that the fax is improving your business efficiency, not impairing it.

Remember too, that there's nothing private about the usual business fax: users of the fax machine at the other end may gleefully read it. Don't put anything confidential or sensitive in a faxed business letter unless you use an encoding facility.

Faxed messages *can* go to the wrong destination. It is sensible to write the recipient's fax number at the top of the page. Include the recipient's first name and surname with the address above the salutation, as you would in any business letter, and your fax will more easily find its way.

Take steps to help effective communication if the fax malfunctions or the recipient's fax runs out of paper: always number the pages, state the total number of pages on the first page, and write 'End' at the foot of the last page. Many business create a fax template with the company name, contact details and set spaces for 'To', 'From' and 'Number of pages'.

Finally, a word about durability. Only a plain-paper fax will produce a copy with lasting properties; the print on thermal fax paper may degenerate seriously over time. This means you may need to follow up a faxed document with a posted copy more suitable for filing.

The following is an example of how to set out a fax.

To:	**Robert Black, Blower Systems**
Fax No:	**(03) 8993 4890**
From:	**Meredith Swain, Chips Pty Ltd**
Fax No:	**(02) 6753 9876**
Date:	**26 January 2007**
Pages:	**2 (including this one)**

Re:	**Samples for your approval**

Dear Robert

Here is the information about the samples you requested.

I'll be in Melbourne from Tuesday until Friday so do try me on the mobile on 0409 654 290 if you need anything else.

Yours sincerely

Meredith Swain

The fax for personal letters

The fax can be ideal for the informal, spontaneous message, and is to the deaf what the phone is to the blind. It's also handy for those who are not computer literate and don't have access to email.

Your mother lives in San Francisco and you suddenly realise that her birthday was yesterday – but she has a fax, so you still have time to compose the birthday ode and send it! You open up the newspaper and discover that a friend has just become a grandfather. His hearing loss means that he can't manage phone calls, but your immediate fax will give him pleasure and his response can be just as rapid. The nice thing about sending a fax for these occasions is that the message is all the more personal for being written in your own hand.

For letters to mark solemn or formal occasions the fax is usually less suitable. This is not just because your words need to be carefully considered. Part of the success of such letters depends on how they are presented: in these situations there is no substitute for the good-quality paper, or the beautiful card that has plenty of space for a short letter. Nor should such significant messages be left to roll out of a fax machine; they should be received in an envelope, in the traditional way. Remember too, that letters written for important occasions are often preserved, and the faxed message is neither a thing of beauty nor (unless the machine is a plain-paper fax) very long lasting.

CHECKLIST

☐ Understand the role of letters in good business and personal communication.

☐ Exploit your fax for letter-writing, but use it wisely.

8

Email

Email (it's jargon for electronic mail) is the term used to describe any letters sent from one computer to another using the internet. Hundreds of millions of messages are sent and received every day all around the world, making it an increasingly important business and personal communication tool.

The huge advantage of email is that it is instant, convenient and private. It is also extremely economical – however long or complicated your message might be, or wherever in the world you may be sending it, it will only cost you the price of a local phone call (and much less if you have access to broadband). It's no wonder that email has become such a crucial addition to both our personal and business communication.

EMAIL ADDRESSES

Before you can send an email, you need to know the recipient's address (also known as a user ID, name or address). This usually takes the following format: name@site.address. The site address usually consists of the name of the service provider, plus either a '.com', and/or the initials of the country from where the email is being sent (e.g. fiona.richards@internet.com.au).

EMAIL ESSENTIALS

Most email software is similar, and you are likely to need to fill in the following boxes when sending a message.

TO: This is the address of the person to whom you are sending the message.

CC: Use this 'carbon copy' function to automatically copy your message to any number of people. However, all recipients will be able to view each other's email addresses, so use this feature with sensitivity.

BCC: The 'blind carbon copy' is the polite option, as recipients will not see the names of other BCC recipients.

SUBJECT: Some systems require that you enter a subject line before your message is sent. Entering a short succinct header lets the recipient know what your message is about – essential for business communications, or if you have some hot gossip for a friend.

WRITING EMAILS

Email writing is really just like any other kind of letter writing. No matter if the message is just a few brief lines, good grammar, spelling and style are still important. Try to be as clear as possible and always re-read for errors before you hit 'send'. Email is instant technology; once sent, there is little you can do to remedy any bad impression caused by sloppy writing.

If you wish to reply to an email you have received, you can simply hit the 'reply' button. Normally, the original message will automatically be incorporated at the bottom of your reply, which is useful when you want to remind someone of what they have written.

When writing emails, keep the body of the text as short as possible. If you need to write a very long message, consider attaching it as a separate file that may be printed out and read at leisure.

Email writing tends to be less formal than standard letter writing, and a number of common abbreviations are used. Use only those symbols that you know the recipient will understand, and don't be tempted to use them inappropriately – within a business letter, for instance. Many of these abbreviations are commonly used for SMS text messages too.

Common abbreviations

AFAICT	as far as I can tell
AFAIK	as far as I know
AIUI	as I understand it
B4	before
BRB	be right back
BTW	by the way
cld	could
doc	document
EOF	end of file
FAQ	frequently asked question
FOC	free of charge
foll	following

Fw:	forwarded message
FWIW	for what it's worth
FYI	for your information
GR8	great
GTG	got to go
HTH	hope this helps
IDTS	I don't think so
IIRC	if I recall correctly
IMHO	in my humble opinion
IMO	in my opinion
IOW	in other words
ITRO	in the region of
LOL	laughing out loud
msg	message
OIC	oh, I see
OTOH	on the other hand
PD	public domain
Re:	reply
ROTFL	rolling on the floor laughing
RTM	read the manual
RU	are you
TBC	to be confirmed
TBD	to be discussed
TIA	thanks in advance

TNX	thanks
UGTBK	you've got to be kidding
WRT	with regard to
YYSSW	yeah, yeah, sure, sure, whatever

Common smileys

:-)	happy
;-)	winking
:-(	sad
:-o	shocked
:-&	tongue-tied
:-P	poking tongue out

Sample business email

From: oliver_clark@sjpv.com.au
To: kylie_swain@business.com
Subject: re: meeting at Talbot's

Hi Kylie

I'll get back to you as soon as I can with the figures on the new account. Timing for the conference call TBC later in the week.

Regards

Oliver

Personal email

From: miffster@email.com
To: stepho@her_best.com
Subject: hot goss

Hello darling. You'll never guess who I ran into at the theatre last night. Louisa Schmidt – remember her from school? She's pregnant, but otherwise looks just the same as ever. She said to say hi to you, and asked after your family. Are you still on for Sat night?
Stepho xxx

CHECKLIST

- Pay attention to grammar, spelling and style, as with any other letter.
- Keep as brief as possible, and consider sending longer documents as an attachment.
- Always re-read before hitting 'send'.
- Use CC and BCC functions appropriately.

9

Letters to Family and Friends

I must answer Lena's letter. She'll think I have forgotten her. I must do it today.
I'll just wait until the weekend.
If I wait a couple more weeks I can wish her a happy birthday.
Oh heavens, I've forgotten Lena's birthday again. I'll write tonight.
I should have written last night. Christmas is coming. I'll send a card then.

Familiar? Of course it is. That's the way friendships sometimes die a slow death. A card at Christmas – if Lena is lucky! Letters and emails to family and friends are great communicators: they can be read and re-read, answered with joy, looked forward,to for days or weeks. And they are not to difficult to write if you use established links as the starting point.

ABSENT FAMILY

You've been thinking of your brother for ages but you have not written to tell him so. You have some photographs of people and places he knows. He lives overseas so it is expensive to keep in touch by phone. Your thoughts go back to your childhood and the very happy times you had on the farm together.

You remember you promised to keep him in touch. For the leisurely communication all this demands, writing an email or letter is the answer. Make up your mind to write *today* and carry out your resolution.

Sit down with pen and paper or at your keyboard and let your thoughts take over. Your brother is at the forefront of your mind, and this will be apparent when you begin to write. Tell him you've been thinking of him constantly, discuss concerns you have in common, remind him of occasions shared, if you miss him say so, tell him you do not want to lose touch because as you are growing older the family is becoming more important to you, and give him news of the family and the work you are doing. Say something about the photos you are sending. Conclude with your love and your hopes of an early reply.

The letter will practically write itself if you concentrate on your brother and share your thoughts and your experiences with him. This will be obvious in your letter.

When your brother answers your letter a marvellous two-way bridge has been set up. All you both have to do is keep walking over it.

DISTANT FRIENDS

Writing to distant friends is not so very different from writing to family, although you may share more of yourself with dear friends than you do with a member of your family. In place of family news you may choose to talk about world events, political events, your work, your holiday, a book you have read recently, a play you have seen, a film you have enjoyed, a new restaurant in your district, or your evening class and the people you meet there. There are endless things to write about if you think of your total environment and the recipient's.

Of course you need not only choose current topics. What about your innermost thoughts. You can share these with a lifelong friend and not feel embarrassed. If you are passionate about the heritage of your city, for example, there's no reason why you can't write about that and your reasons for holding such strong opinions. If you believe that the country is going rapidly to the dogs you can write about that in paragraphs that might scorch the paper. You are expressing yourself and making someone else aware of your emotions. This is no bad thing: when feelings are bottled up, letters and emails can be a safety valve. The world of literature is full of collections of letters in which innermost thoughts make timeless reading.

You're not expecting to be published. But you *are* hoping to keep those lines of communication open to your friends, and this is a good way to do it. We all have interesting thoughts, and even if our letters do not read like Virginia Woolf's or George Bernard Shaw's, our personal reflections are still worth setting down on paper.

It's quite possible to conduct a stimulating argument over email or via the post, and it is often the differences in friendships that keep them important to us. We don't have to enjoy all the same things to be friends, nor have the same tenets. The enthusiasm of the disparate views expressed in the messages received make them wonderful to read.

Receiving a good letter is still one of the pleasures of life, and the written word may be more eloquent than the spoken. A letter really is a more lasting expression of friendship than any conversation. Happily, there are many friendships that endure because writing has been recognised as an important way of carrying on a conversation over long stretches of time or distance.

GOOD COMMUNICATIONS

One of the secrets of writing a good letter or email is to make sure that it conveys your personality. Another important element is detail: an informative piece of writing is always more satisfying to read than a short, perfunctory note.

A poor email

In the following email to parents living in another state, Kylie includes news and asks a question, but it is not a great communication.

Dear Mum and Dad
I hope you are both well. We are. The children have had a few colds through the winter but are better now.

The wildflowers are lovely.

We had Roxanne and Harry to stay for a few days last week. It was good to see them.

The weather has been fine and warm. Soon of course it will be hot enough to swim, so we look forward to that. The twins are swimming quite well.

Are you coming over for Christmas?

Lots of love
Kylie

Kylie's email was not very startling or informative, was it? Let's see if we can make it a little more human; somehow put Kylie right in there, so that her personality comes home to Mum and Dad more forcibly.

A better email

Dear Mum and Dad

I hope you are both well. We are. The children have had some nasty colds during the winter, but are feeling (and looking) better now. They didn't miss very much school, and as you know that's important to them at their stage of education.

You should see the wildflowers this spring! They are just glorious. In Bush Park one side of the road is smothered with them, and the other is much more sparse. This is because one side of the road had a bushfire last summer, and the seeds have all germinated with the heat. Perhaps we should think about controlled burns each summer? It could make a spectacular difference.

We had Roxanne and Harry to stay for a few days last week. It was good to see them. It's four years since they were last in Australia. Doesn't time rush by? Roxanne has a new job: she is now head designer for a casual wear company in Bushnell, and she loves it. Harry is still working as a civil engineer, but is not so busy on the consulting side as he was. They say that business in England is slowly picking up, but they have all experienced a downturn, with some firms declaring themselves bankrupt rather than continuing to struggle. Quite like us really.

The weather has been fine and warm, so it won't be long before we are all on the beach again. The twins are swimming rather well now. I am being modest on their behalf; they are swimming really well, and competing against each other quite happily. At the school sports in October their teacher expects them to win their age races. She won't say whether Grace or Julia will be in front. I couldn't tell you either – they are neck and neck at most training sessions. Isn't it good to see them taking after their mother? I now appreciate how hard it was for you to get up early every morning for me. I didn't think much about it then, but a similar experience certainly brings it home.

Are you coming over for Christmas? I do hope you are, because it would make our festivities so much more exciting. There's no one quite like Gran and Gramps in the kids' eyes – and in ours! Please think about it, and book early for the best deal for seats on the plane. I'll make your special Christmas cake recipe for you. How's that for bribery and corruption?

Michael sends his love, so do the children, and of course so do I.

Love as always
Kylie

There is a vast difference, isn't there? It's not hard to see why.

Kylie has taken more time. She has thought about her parents and their interests, giving them news about mutual friends and painting a word-picture of Bush Park and its wildflowers, with a few thoughts about controlled burning as well. She has told them news of their grandchildren. She has made her parents feel wanted for Christmas and has reminded them of their sacrifices for her. Her warmth of feeling is obvious throughout the whole email.

In the poor email, the weather, the wildflowers, the visitors and the grandchildren all rate a mention and the invitation is issued for Christmas, but without any real feeling that Kylie would like her parents to be with her. The good email is likely to receive an instant response, with Gran and Gramps responding to the warm invitation to spend Christmas with their grandchildren.

Try to imagine your feelings if you were to receive the first type of email from a friend or family member. Contrast that with the emotions you would feel if an email like the second popped into your inbox. That really sums up your opportunities as a writer of personal communications. All it takes is a little more thought, a little more time, and a little more of feelings expressed; the rest takes care of itself.

BEWARE THE ROUND ROBIN

So there you are – your new letter-writing skills leading to an upsurge in your correspondence.

Let's hope that your newfound confidence won't lead you to write the kind of 'round robin' letter that seems to come more and more frequently with Christmas cards. You know the sort of thing. A bland, uninteresting account of what has happened to the family over the past year (usually seen through rose-coloured glasses: Emily failed her exam, but is pleased to have another year of study as she feels she needs it; Franco was made redundant in February, and is finding new hobbies).

There's little intimacy in these letters, for they are written for friends and acquaintances scattered around the globe. They must of necessity be generally directed, just skim the surface, tell all in a few words and thus lose all spontaneity. Usually too they are written in the third person, so they have an impersonal sound to them. You don't find the person you know on the page, as you do with a personal letter coming only to you or your family.

So take time for the personally directed letter. It is an art, and should be nourished as all arts are, for they add colour and flavour to life. The warmth, the depth, the feeling, the commitment that goes into a good personal letter is incomparable.

CHECKLIST

- [ ] Don't procrastinate – write today!
- [ ] Take time to think yourself into the mind of the recipient.
- [ ] Share your thoughts and news.
- [ ] Establish two-way communication.
- [ ] Put something of yourself onto each page.

10
. . . .
Letters to the Editor

Letters to the Editor appear in newspapers and magazines all over the world.
Often they form a section that readers peruse the moment they open the paper,
for they can be argumentative, confrontational, opinionated, thought provoking,
prejudiced, informative or amusing. They form a lively page of any newspaper
and, as letters received from the public, they give the paper a human face.

TYPES OF LETTERS
Roughly, letters written to newspapers fall into four categories:

- ▶ a letter to open an argument about a particular issue
- ▶ a letter that takes a different viewpoint from one already published
- ▶ a letter from a community group looking for a forum
- ▶ an all-embracing letter, usually of thanks or appreciation.

On a particular day, the Letters to the Editor in *The Age* newspaper included the
following topics.

- Private schools should have their subsidies cut.
- Industrial change is sorely needed in the State of Victoria.
- The homeless will suffer because of special schools' closures.
- Science should learn that politics is about giving as well as taking.
- The sometimes harmful effects of childhood vaccination.
- Federal money being unwisely spent in the suburbs.
- Does the police force need to question young people so often?
- A disgruntled motorist's view on unlicensed road users – joggers, cyclists and the like.

Most letters fell into the category of taking a different viewpoint from an article or letter already published. The disgruntled motorist was opening an argument, for the runners and cyclists are bound to defend their right to use the roads too. The grandmother who wrote about the dangers of some vaccines for babies was putting an opinion and using her experience and that of her daughter. Clearly she is one of a group in the community looking for a forum.

There wasn't an all-embracing letter in the correspondence published by *The Age* that day, so here is an example of one that might have been written on behalf of a large charity organisation immediately after its annual appeal had been conducted.

On behalf of Hard Times Ahead I wish to thank, through your columns, the large band of volunteers who helped with the Give More Appeal on Saturday April 27. In the present economic climate the demand for our services is huge, and we are even more dependent on the money collected during the appeal. On Saturday volunteers collecting in the streets faced unusually cold and wet conditions, yet there was a record turnout. Other aspects of the appeal were equally well supported by volunteers ready to tackle any task, however unfamiliar.

Their efforts were much appreciated by Hard Times Ahead. It is heartening to see such a positive community response, particularly from young people. As a result of the volunteers' willing efforts a large sum of money will be available to help those in need.

Elizabeth Costas, Appeal Coordinator

All-embracing letters often relate directly to local situations; if this is the case, your regional newspaper is the right forum.

IS IT FOR YOU?

Consider the following if you are thinking of writing to the Editor.

▶ Look at the types of letters published. Is your issue one to which the newspaper might give space?
▶ Are you able to write succinctly? No paper will print a verbose argument, as space has to be rationed so that as many people as possible can have letters published. Evan a short letter may be cut.

- ▶ Are you prepared to sign your name? If not, forget it. The courage of your convictions must be uppermost, and you name must be published (or at least provided) to cover legalities.
- ▶ Are you planning to attack the issue the journalist wrote about, and not the journalist? Can you name the date of the article and then list your reasons for disagreeing?
- ▶ Are you planning to avoid acronyms and abbreviations, so that the reader will easily understand what you are saying?
- ▶ Can you type or email your letter, or handwrite clearly? If your letter can't be deciphered, you might as well save the effort. Your letter may be misread by a subeditor and the meaning changed. You don't want that happening, especially as your letter will become public property.

Think carefully if the idea of your letter becoming public property makes you pause. You might do better to express your displeasure to the person or organisation concerned than to have your letter published and then regret that it was placed on so many breakfast tables.

THE FORUM

Difficulties aside, a chance to have your say and air your views is something to be cherished. A letter to the Editor can also be a way of influencing public thinking and helping to bring about social reform. Taking part in such a forum can bring a great deal of satisfaction.

Happily, not all letters to newspapers need to be serious. Some of the light-hearted and long-running debates conducted through the Letters to the Editor are fun to take part in, and enormous fun to read with your toast and coffee.

CHECKLIST

- Study the letters published in the newspaper of your choice.
- Type if possible, or write clearly.
- Express yourself succinctly.
- Attack the issue, not the writer.
- You must give your name.
- Remember that your thoughts, once published, are public property.

11

Answering Back

Answering a letter ought to be easy, but very often it is not. Procrastination makes it harder: the first flush of pleasure at hearing from someone has dissipated, other busy-ness has taken over, and a precious link with someone is in danger of being lost. Don't let this happen: answer your letters within a few weeks at the very latest, emails even sooner.

SITTING DOWN TO IT

Make up your mind to write on a particular day, even at a particular time of day if that helps your resolve. Organise what you need in advance – suitable writing materials, stamps, a fresh printer cartridge. Set yourself up to your satisfaction, on the veranda on a Sunday morning, with a pot of coffee, or at the computer while the baby is asleep. Put the letter to be answered before you, or re-read the email you received.

THE TWO-WAY LINE

Why do you need the letter beside you, or the email on the screen? You read the letter when you received it, shared it with others, re-read it once, but then you put it away and the contents are no longer fresh in your mind. Having the letter with you means that you are able to answer questions or comment on the subjects raised by your correspondent. In this way, the letter becomes a two-way conversation. Without the letter as a trigger, your reply will not be complete, and it will therefore be not so satisfactory to its recipient.

Not all letter writers (indeed very few) keep copies of their correspondence, so you should *never* write an answer like this one.

Question 1: Yes.
Question 2: No.
Question 3: Maybe.
Question 4: Perhaps.
Question 5: Next week.

The exception is if you are exchanging emails, and both have saved copies of your correspondence. Or better yet, include the text from the previous email in your reply.

For letters, always reply to the questions in context.

You were asking if I still see Gina, and yes I am happy to say that I do. Do we intend to get married? No, we don't at this stage, though one never knows. There may be opposition to the idea anyway, because her family is rather traditional and would not like her to marry outside the Italian community. I'll tackle that problem if or when it arises.

You wanted to know if my job would be taking me overseas this year, and I'm not sure how to answer that question. There is a distinct possibility of this happening, but I will not know until May. Even then, there is an element of uncertainty because of the present economic climate. As to changing my job, I cannot see this happening in the foreseeable future, again because of the economic climate. In my field there seems to be more firing than hiring, so I am consolidating my position, working hard and getting the results on the board – just like you did, Mum.

This two-way business is highly satisfactory when it is handled in this manner. Always try to answer queries, for they are the crux of the letter very often. If someone is interested enough in you to write a letter, that someone really wants to have the answers. Don't think of it as prying; it is a genuine desire to learn of your movements and to share with you the joys and sorrows and achievements of life. Make sure that you include in your letter some news of your own or open some topic to be discussed, so that your correspondent has something to write about when replying.

FIRST SENTENCES

Don't always start with 'Thank you for your letter' or 'Hope this reply finds you well as it does me'. There are clichés in writing that should be avoided as there are in speech. There is nothing to stop you being appreciative, but don't make it the opening remark if you want to hold the attention of the recipient. It will be glossed over while the reader looks for some news. A weather report is acceptable in your letter, but it certainly shouldn't be the focal point. If you've suffered the effects of a cyclone, an earthquake, a severe hailstorm or a flash flood, by all means use that as your reason for writing the letter. Anything less can be merely boring.

If you use the weather as a springboard to something else, that's ideal. For example: 'Spring has arrived, and the garden is blooming'. Then go on to describe your garden, so that the reader of the letter may imagine its glory and perfumes. Or perhaps something like this: 'We are having a very cold winter this year, so the fire has been going every night. There I am chopping wood – splendid for getting me warm!' Those few words conjure up all sorts of images, and could well lead on to an anecdote or three.

YOU'VE WON

The main idea behind these few notes is to have you answering your mail. Writing a letter or email and receiving no response can be devastating, for it is a form of rejection. Meaning to answer is not good enough; do it! You will feel virtuous and the person who receives your answer will be delighted. So it's an all-win situation, and it's one well within your capabilities.

CHECKLIST

- Answer letters and emails promptly.
- Set a day and time to do it – and stick to your schedule.
- Try to begin in an interesting fashion.
- Respond to all questions in context.
- Include news and enquiries of your own, to invite a further letter.
- Unless there has been a natural disaster, avoid too much about the weather.

12
· · · · · · · · · · · ·
Wrapping it Up

Addressing an envelope may seem like the simplest aspect of letter writing, but it can be complicated. People have different titles, and there are specific modes for addressing the envelope of a letter. Over the years there have been changes, so it pays to be a little more careful than you may at first think is necessary.

PLEASING THE RECIPIENT

Social change has led to changes in how we address people with whom we are communicating by writing. For example, it was once customary for letters addressed to a couple to have on the envelope only the wife's name. It was assumed that she would be keeping the home fires burning and would thus be able to open the letter first then share the contents with her husband when he came back from a hard day's hunting and gathering. Now you may address the envelope to them both, or to one or the other. It is also correct to write 'Mrs V. and Mr B. Placzek', instead of the older form, 'Mr and Mrs B. Placzek'.

Another change is the increasingly common practice of writing only the person's given name and surname, for example 'Hermione Morgan'. The 'Mrs', 'Miss' or 'Ms' has been dropped. However this is not a practice that pleases some older people. They may take exception to being addressed as 'Ms' or assume the writer lacks respect because they use a given name without any prefix at all.

Perhaps a good general rule for writing to older people is not to address an envelope baldly, and to establish what prefix the recipient prefers. This situation is complicated by the fact that some people prefer not to have prefixes or titles, or even surnames, on envelopes addressed to them in private correspondence.

Email is another matter entirely, as the address is set and you need only worry about how you salute the person to whom you are writing.

What has happened is that social change has opened a lively can of worms, and until the writhing and squirming is over you need to know how to deal with the problems created.

MALES

In the past, when writing to a boy up to nine or ten years old it was customary to address the envelope 'Master Timothy McDougall'. Now 'Master' has been dropped and it is acceptable to write 'Timothy McDougall'. Once a young man was 'of age' it was correct to then use 'Mr Timothy McDougall'. 'Mr' is a form of respect that is still used, and stays with a man for life unless he has some other title, which is covered later in this chapter.

The use of 'Esq.' after a man's name instead of 'Mr' has largely disappeared, perhaps because it was so often used incorrectly. Officially and correctly it was used when addressing envelopes to Commanders, Companions, Officers and Members of the various Orders of Chivalry (that is, Australian and British honours). For example, the holder of an AM was addressed, if male, as Michael Hanrahan Esq., AM.

Others entitled to use 'Esquire' included holders of senior positions under the Crown: State and Federal members of Parliament, permanent heads of Commonwealth departments, chairmen of statutory authorities, barristers-at-law, and justices of the peace.

Modern usage seems to be dropping these distinctions entirely, though in official mail from a State Government House the custom is still upheld. The Governor-General's office would still use the same set of guidelines.

FEMALES

For a female there are more choices. It used to be just 'Miss' until a girl married, and thereafter 'Mrs' – unless there was a special title of some kind. Now that simplicity has been shattered by the introduction of 'Ms'. This is now widely used and completely acceptable. It makes a great deal of sense because it de-emphasises a woman's marital status, and saves some embarrassment when it is not known whether a woman is married or not. At the same time, if a married woman chooses to be called 'Mrs' she is entitled to that, and if she chooses to use her husband's name, that is still acceptable.

For written forms of address, many married women now prefer to use their given name, so that they do not appear an appendage of their husbands. Thus it is common to find 'Mrs (or 'Ms') Helen Zimmerman' on an envelope, instead of 'Mrs Gordon Zimmerman'. It is also quite acceptable for a married woman to retain her maiden name, so that she is seen as a person in her own right.

Furthermore it used to be always 'Mrs John Brownlee' until John died or until John and Jane divorced. Then the correct address on the envelope was 'Mrs Jane Brownlee' indicating that the woman was widowed or divorced. To complicate matters further, a widow had a choice of continuing to be 'Mrs John Brownlee' if she wished, but a divorced woman did not.

These distinctions now seem archaic, but they must be recognised because many older people like to retain them. They are doing what they were taught was correct and are happy with it. If in doubt, always opt for the more formal approach, as you are far less likely to cause offence.

DIGNITARIES

If you are involved in community projects, or work to bring about social reform, you will have occasion to write to various dignitaries. Here's how you address them in writing.

Australian leaders

Correspondence to the Prime Minister of Australia is addressed 'The Right Honourable the Prime Minister, Mr (or Ms) ...', and a State Premier as 'The Honourable ...', MP (the abbreviation the 'The Hon.' is acceptable).

The Governor-General's correspondence is sent to 'The Private Secretary to His (or Her) Excellence the Governor-General of Australia'. State Governors may be written to directly, so you should address it to 'His Excellency, Sir …' or 'His Excellency Admiral …' or 'Her Excellency Ms ….' (add the Governor's given name and surname), Governor of … (add the name of the State).

The Administrator of a Territory is addressed 'His (or Her) Honour …' (add the Administrator's given name and surname), Administrator of the Northern Territory (or whatever applies).

Parliamentarians

Cabinet ministers in the Commonwealth Senate, if Privy Counsellors, are addressed 'Senator the Right Honourable P. J. Fisclini, Minister of State for …'. If Cabinet Ministers are not Privy Counsellors, the mode of address is 'Senator the Honourable S. J. Hahndorf, Minister of State for …'.

Cabinet ministers in the House of Representatives follow the same forms of address if entitled to the prefix 'Honourable'. The address for members of the Senate who are not entitled to 'Honourable' is 'Senator P. Q. Chua'. In the House of Representatives if the recipient is not entitled to a prefix, the envelope bears the address 'M. Z. Hopetoun Esq., MP'.

In State parliaments Cabinet ministers' and presiding officers' correspondence is addressed 'The Honourable J. S. Hames, MLC, Minister of …'. Members of the Legislative Council are addressed 'The Honourable T. E. O'Shea, MLC'.

If they are not entitled to the prefix 'Honourable', the address is 'Ms Katherine van Hoven, MP' or 'J. L. Smythe, Esq., MP.'

British titles

Should you be moved to write to a member of the British Royal family or peerage, you will find much helpful detail in *Debrett's Correct Form* or *Debrett's Peerage and Baronetage*.

The judiciary

If the Chief Justice or a judge of the High Court of Australia is a knight or a Privy Counsellor the envelope should be addressed 'The Right Honourable Sir Rollo Elliott', and if the recipient is not, the form is 'The Honourable Justice Elliott'. This form of address is retained into retirement. This applies more particularly in Victoria, where the Governor may ask the British monarch to grant this form of address to a judge upon retirement from the Supreme Court of the State. This discretion may also be applied to members of the Legislative Council of Victoria after ten years' service, or to the President of the Legislative Council or the Speaker of the Legislative Assembly after having served three years in their respective offices in Victoria.

In most State Supreme Courts the envelope is addressed to 'The Honourable Sir Alfred Fetke or 'The Honourable Mr Justice Fetke' – the only difference being the title appropriate to a knighthood. For South Australia, however, the mode of address is 'The Honourable Justice Wilson'. In County Courts any correspondence goes to 'His Honour Judge Hanniford'.

If you are writing to a female judge you may need to check first with the court concerned, particularly about the correct prefix if the court requires one.

Local government

Writing to members of local government can be a little complicated because different capital cities in Australia have different requirements.

Lord mayors of Sydney, Hobart and Brisbane are addressed 'The Right Honourable the Lord Mayor of ..., Alderman F. Grioli. A letter to the Lord Mayor of Melbourne is addressed to 'The Right Honourable the Lord Mayor of Melbourne, Councillor B. Smith'. Letters to the lord mayors of Adelaide and Perth are addressed to: 'The Right Honourable the Lord Mayor of ..., Mr R. Joubert'. For the cities of Newcastle in New South Wales and Geelong in Victoria, the correct way of addressing the envelope is (respectively) 'The Right Worshipful the Lord Mayor of Newcastle, Alderman K. Emm', and 'The Right Worshipful the Mayor of Geelong, Councillor N. Gee'. The forms for addressing an envelope need no adjustment when the Lord Mayor is a woman, as the term 'Lord Mayor' does not suppose one gender or the other.

Correspondence to the Lady Mayoress in the capital cities and Newcastle is addressed 'The Lady Mayoress of ..., Ms S. Smith'. For Geelong the correct form of address is 'The Mayoress of Geelong, Mrs J. Jones'. You should ascertain what prefix the Lady Mayoress prefers, for example 'Ms' or 'Mrs' or 'Dr'.

In other cities, towns and boroughs the envelope for a mayor is addressed to 'Councillor O. Ivanov, Mayor of the City of …'. Shire presidents should be addressed 'Councillor D. Kanacki, President of the Shire of …'.

Should you need to write to a member of the diplomatic or consular service there is a correct form for this too. Letters to High Commissioners and ambassadors are addressed 'His Excellency Mr J. Fanella, Ambassador of …' or 'High Commissioner for …'. For a consul-general or consul the address should be written as 'P. Rigo Esq., Consul-General of Australia to Utopia'.

The clergy

For the clergy, there is usually a difference between what is written on an invitation and what appears on the envelope. The advice below also needs to be adapted where clergy are female.

Anglican Church of Australia

For an archbishop:
▶ the invitation – 'The Archbishop of … (add name of archdiocese, for example New City) and Mrs Brown'
▶ the envelope – 'The Most Reverend W. Brown, Archbishop of New City'

For a bishop:
▶ the invitation – 'The Bishop of … (add name of diocese) and Mrs Rose'
▶ the envelope – 'The Right Reverend Mr P. Rose, Bishop of Winterton'

For a dean:

- ▶ the invitation – 'The Dean of ... (add name of diocese) and Mrs Black'
- ▶ the envelope – 'The Very Reverend J. Black, Dean of Summerdale'

For a canon:

- ▶ the invitation – 'The Reverend Canon and Mrs A. White'
- ▶ the envelope – 'The Reverend Canon A. White'

For other members of the Anglican clergy:

- ▶ the invitation – 'The Reverend G. and Mrs Green'
- ▶ the envelope – 'The Reverend G. Green'

Roman Catholic Church

For an archbishop:

- ▶ the invitation – 'His Grace the Most Reverend M. Sheedy'
- ▶ the envelope – 'His Grace the Most Reverend M. Sheedy, Archbishop of Forest City'

For a bishop:

- ▶ the invitation – 'His Lordship, the Most Reverend N. O'Shea, Bishop of Mountainville'
- ▶ the envelope – 'His Lordship, the Most Reverend N. O'Shea, Bishop of Mountainville'

Uniting Church

For the moderator:

▶ the invitation – 'The Moderator and Mrs Herring'
▶ the envelope – 'The Reverend L. Herring, Moderator of the Uniting Church in Australia (Synod of …)'

If the moderator is a lay person the envelope should be addressed 'L. Herring Esq.' if a man, and the preferred form of address if a woman.

Other Christian Churches

▶ the invitation – 'The Reverend C. and Mrs Kokas'
▶ the envelope – 'The Reverend C. Kokas'

Jewish Congregation

For a rabbi:

▶ the invitation – 'Rabbi S. and Mrs Bayer'
▶ the envelope – 'Rabbi S. Bayer'

Note: Always check that the wife of a clergyman wishes to be known as 'Mrs'. She may, for instance, be entitled to the prefix 'Dr' and prefer to use it. She may have adopted 'Ms' and wish that to be used at all times, or she may be using her maiden name. Likewise, the male spouse of a female religious official may have his own preferences. These differences you can usually check with the office or secretary of the religious organisation involved.

Whew! What a list! As the old adage says, 'If a thing is worth doing it's worth doing well', so you might as well have all the information at the flick of a page.

PLEASING THE MACHINE

Australia Post stresses the importance of including the postcode and positioning it correctly on any envelope you address. As well, Australia Post encourages letter-writers to eliminate any end-of-line punctuation from addresses. Both these measures allow letters to be electronically sorted.

Leaving out superfluous punctuation makes good sense, but it may be difficult to remember if you have been in the habit of using commas and full stops after names, addresses and towns. Punctuation is usually used to make a meaning on the page quite clear. However, when it comes to writing an address on an envelope, those end-of-line commas and stops are not necessary. Look at the example of Australia Post's recommended style, which follows. The address is certainly as clear as in the older, punctuated style. The layout does all that is needed, for the punctuation really did not serve any purpose (though note that full stops may still appear after the addressee's initials, but are not used with 'LSD' or similar abbreviations). .

Mr S. J. Jonas
Managing Director
LSD Ltd
27 Dandenong Road
DANDENONG VIC

3 1 7 5

While salutations at the beginning and end of letters, as well as addresses written at the top, now follow the same trend of omitting end-of-line punctuation, of course you still need punctuation in the body of your letter or email: the recipient needs to be able to follow your thoughts easily and good punctuation will make all the difference.

CHECKLIST

☐ Familiarise yourself with older and newer ways of addressing people.

☐ Think about how the recipient of your communication would like to be addressed.

☐ Be aware that there are correct forms for addressing letters to dignitaries.

☐ Omit end-of-line punctuation when addressing an envelope.

☐ Remember the postcode.

Australian Postcodes

The following postcode ranges are allocated to the states and territories:

New South Wales and Australian Capital Territory	2000–2999
New South Wales private boxes	1000–1999
Victoria	3000–3999
Queensland	4000–4999
South Australia	5000–5999
Western Australia	6000–6999
Tasmania	7000–7999
Northern Territory	0800–0899

Applecross 6953
Applethorpe 4378
Apslawn 7190
Apsley 3319
Apsley 7030
Araluen 2622
Araluen 4570
Aramac 4726
Arana Hills 4054
Aranbanga 4625
Aranda 2614
Ararat 3377
Aratula 4309
Arcadia 2159
Arcadia 3613
Arcadia 4819
Arcadia Vale 2283
Archer 0830
Archerfield 4108
Archies Creek 3995
Ardath 6419
Ardeer 3022
Ardglen 2338
Ardmona 3629
Ardross 6153
Ardrossan 5571
Areegra 3480
Areyonga 0872
Argenton 2284
Argents Hill 2449
Argyle 4721
Argyle 6239
Ariah Park 2665
Armadale 3143
Armadale 6112
Armadale 6992
Armadale North 3143
Armatree 2831

Armidale 2350
Armstrong Beach 4737
Armstrong Creek 4520
Arncliffe 2205
Arno Bay 5603
Arnold 3551
Aroona 4551
Arrawarra Headland 2456
Arrino 6519
Arrowsmith 6525
Arrowsmith East 6519
Artarmon 1570
Artarmon 2064
Arthur River 6315
Arthur River 7330
Arthurs Creek 3099
Arthurs Seat 3936
Arthurton 5572
Arthurville 2820
Arundel 4214
Ascot 3364
Ascot 4007
Ascot 4359
Ascot 6104
Ascot Park 5043
Ascot Vale 3032
Ashbourne 3442
Ashbourne 5157
Ashburton 3147
Ashbury 2193
Ashby 6065
Ashcroft 2168
Ashendon 6111
Ashfield 1800
Ashfield 2131
Ashfield 4670
Ashfield 6054
Ashford 2361

Ashford 5035
Ashgrove 4060
Ashley 2400
Ashmont 2650
Ashmore 4214
Ashton 5137
Ashtonfield 2323
Ashwood 3147
Aspendale 3195
Aspendale Gardens 3195
Aspley 4034
Asquith 2077
Athelstone 5076
Atherton 4883
Athlone 3818
Athol 4350
Athol Park 5012
Attadale 6156
Attunga 2345
Attwood 3049
Atwell 6164
Aubin Grove 6164
Auburn 1835
Auburn 2144
Auburn 3123
Auburn 5451
Auchenflower 4066
Auchmore 3570
Audley 2232
Augathella 4477
Augusta 6290
Augustine Heights 4300
Auldana 5072
Aurukun 4871
Austinmer 2515
Austins Ferry 7011
Austinville 4213
Austral 2179
Australia Square 1215

Australian Defence
Forces 2890
Australian National
University 0200
Australind 6233
Avalon Beach 2107
Avenel 3664
Avenell Heights 4670
Avenue Range 5273
Avoca 2577
Avoca 3467
Avoca 4670
Avoca 7213
Avoca Beach 2251
Avoca Vale 4306
Avondale 4670
Avondale Heigts 3034
Avonsleigh 3782
Awaba 2283
Axedale 3551
Ayers Rock 0872
Aylmerton 2575
Ayr 4807

B
Baan Baa 2390
Baandee 6412
Baarmutha 3747
Babakin 6428
Babbage Island 6701
Babinda 4861
Bacchus Marsh 3340
Back Creek 2484
Backmede 2470
Baddaginnie 3670
Badebup 6317
Baden 7120
Badgerin Rock 6475
Badgerys Creek 2555

Badgin 6302
Badgingarra 6521
Badjaling 6383
Badu Island 4875
Baerami Creek 2333
Baffle Creek 4674
Baffle West 4454
Bagdad 7030
Bagnoo 2446
Bagot 0820
Bahrs Scrub 4207
Bailieston 3608
Bairnsdale 3875
Bajool 4699
Bakers Creek 4740
Bakers Hill 6562
Bakers Swamp 2820
Bakery Hill 3354
Bakewell 0832
Balaclava 3183
Balaklava 5461
Balbarrup 6258
Balberra 4740
Balcatta 6021
Balcatta 6914
Bald Hills 4036
Bald Ridge 2795
Baldivis 6171
Baldry 2867
Balga 6061
Balgowan 4401
Balgowan 5573
Balgowlah 2093
Balgownie 2519
Balhannah 5242
Balickera 2324
Balingup 6253
Balkuling 6383
Balla Balla 6714

Balladong 6302
Balladonia 6443
Balladoran 2831
Ballajura 6066
Ballalaba 2622
Ballan 3342
Ballandean 4382
Ballarat 3350
Ballarat Mail Centre
  private boxes 3354
Ballarat private boxes
  3353
Ballarat roadside
  delivery 3352
Ballard 4352
Ballaying 6315
Balldale 2646
Ballengarra 2441
Balliang 3340
Ballidu 6606
Ballimore 2830
Ballina 2478
Ballogie 4610
Bally Bally 6304
Ballyroe 2795
Balmain 2041
Balmattum 3666
Balmoral 2283
Balmoral 3407
Balmoral 4171
Balmoral Ridge 4552
Balmoral Village 2571
Balnagowan 4740
Balnarring 3926
Balook 3971
Balranald 2715
Balwyn 3103
Balwyn North 3104
Bamaga 4876

Bamarang 2540
Bamawm 3561
Bamboo Creek 4860
Bambra 3241
Bambun 6503
Ban Ban 4625
Ban Ban Springs 4625
Banana 4702
Bandiana 3694
Bandon Grove 2420
Bandy Creek 6450
Bandya 6440
Bangalee 2541
Bangalee 4703
Bangalow 2479
Bangholme 3175
Bangor 2234
Bangor 7267
Banjup 6164
Banks 2906
Banks Creek 4306
Banks Pocket 4570
Banksa Grove 6031
Banksia 2216
Banksia Beach 4507
Banksia Park 5091
Banksiadale 6213
Banksmeadow 2019
Bankstown 1885
Bankstown 2200
Bannister 2580
Bannister 6390
Bannockburn 3331
Bannockburn 4207
Banora Point 2486
Banyena 3388
Banyo 4014
Banyule 3084
Bapaume 4352

Bar Beach 2300
Baradine 2396
Baraimal 2470
Baralaba 4702
Barambah 4601
Baranduda 3691
Barbalin 6479
Barberton 6510
Barcaldine 4725
Barden Ridge 2234
Bardon 4065
Bardwell Park 2207
Bardwell Valley 2207
Baree 4714
Bareena 3220
Barellan 2665
Barellan Point 4306
Bargara 4670
Bargo 2574
Barham 2732
Baringhup 3463
Barker Creek Flat 4615
Barkers Creek 3451
Barkly 3381
Barkstead 3352
Barlil 4605
Barlows Hill 4703
Barlyne 4625
Barmah 3639
Barmaryee 4703
Barmedman 2668
Barmera 5345
Barmoya 4703
Barnadown 3557
Barnard 4702
Barnawartha 3688
Barnes Bay 7150
Barney Point 4680
Barnsley 2278

Barongarook 3249
Barooga 3644
Barraba 2347
Barrabool 3221
Barrabup 6275
Barrack Heights 2528
Barrack Point 2528
Barragga Bay 2546
Barragup 6210
Barramornie 4416
Barramunga 3249
Barratta 4809
Barrengarry 2577
Barretta 7054
Barrine 4872
Barringha 4816
Barrington 2422
Barrington 7306
Barringun 2840
Barringun 4490
Barron 4878
Barrow Creek 0872
Barrow Island 6712
Barry 2799
Bartle Frere 4861
Barton 2600
Barunah Park 3329
Barwon Downs 3243
Barwon Heads 3227
Baryulgil 2460
Basilisk 4871
Basin Pocket 4305
Basin View 2540
Baskerville 6056
Basket Range 5138
Bass 3991
Bass Hill 2197
Bassendean 2365
Bassendean 6054

Bassendean 6934
Batchelor 0845
Bateau Bay 2261
Batehaven 2536
Bateman 6150
Batemans Bay 2536
Batesford 3221
Bathurst 2795
Batlow 2730
Battery Hill 4551
Battery Point 7004
Baudin 6284
Bauhinia 4718
Baulkham Hills 1755
Baulkham Hills 2153
Bauple 4650
Bawley Point 2539
Baxter 3911
Bay Village 2261
Bayindeen 3375
Bayles 3981
Baynton 6714
Bayonet Head 6330
Bayrick 4478
Bayswater 3153
Bayswater 6053
Bayswater 6933
Bayswater North 3153
Bayview 2104
Bayview Heights 4868
Beachlands 6530
Beachmere 4510
Beachport 5280
Beacon 6472
Beacon Hill 2100
Beaconsfield 2015
Beaconsfield 3807
Beaconsfield 4740
Beaconsfield 6162

Beaconsfield 7270
Beaconsfield Upper 3808
Beadell 6440
Bealiba 3475
Beaudesert 4285
Beaufort 3373
Beaufort River 6394
Beaumaris 3193
Beaumaris 7215
Beaumont 2577
Beaumont 5066
Beaumont 6450
Beaumont Hills 2155
Beauty Point 2546
Beauty Point 7270
Beaver Rock 4650
Beckenham 6107
Beckom 2665
Bedford 6052
Bedford Park 5042
Bedfordale 6112
Bedgerebong 2871
Bedourie 4829
Beeac 3251
Beebo 4385
Beech Forest 3237
Beechboro 6063
Beechford 7252
Beechina 6556
Beechmont 4211
Beechwood 2446
Beechworth 3747
Beecroft 2119
Beela 6224
Beelbangera 2680
Beelbi Creek 4659
Beelerup 6239
Beeliar 6164
Beenaam Valley 4570

Beenleigh 4207
Beenong 6353
Beerburrum 4517
Beermulla 6503
Beeron 4626
Beerwah 4519
Bega 2550
Beilba 4454
Bejoording 6566
Belair 5052
Belbora 2422
Belconnen 2617
Belconnen private boxes
    2616
Beldon 6027
Belfield 2191
Belford 2335
Belgian Gardens 4810
Belgrave 3160
Belhus 6055
Belivah 4207
Bell 2786
Bell 4408
Bell Bay 7253
Bell Park 3215
Bell Post Hill 3215
Bella Creek 4570
Bella Vista 2153
Bellamack 0832
Bellambi 2518
Bellangry 2446
Bellara 4507
Bellarine 3221
Bellata 2397
Bellawongarah 2535
Bellbird 2325
Bellbird Park 4300
Bellbowrie 4070
Bellbrae 3228

Bellbridge 3691
Bellbrook 2440
Bellenden Ker 4871
Bellerive 7018
Bellevue 6056
Bellevue Heights 5050
Bellevue Hill 2023
Bellimbopinni 2440
Bellingen 2454
Bellingham 7254
Bells Creek 4551
Belmont 2280
Belmont 3216
Belmont 4153
Belmont 6104
Belmont 6984
Belmore 2192
Belmunda 4740
Belrose 2085
Beltana 5730
Belvedere 4860
Belvedere Park 3198
Bemboka 2550
Bemm River 3889
Ben Lomond 2365
Bena 3946
Benair 4610
Benalla 3672
Benalla private boxes
    3671
Benambra 3900
Benandarah 2536
Benaraby 4680
Benarkin 4306
Benayeo 3319
Bencubbin 6477
Bend of Islands 3097
Bendalong 2539
Bendemeer 2355

Bendick Murrell 2803
Bendigo 3550
Bendigo Mail Centre
    private boxes 3554
Bendigo private boxes
    3552
Bendoc 3888
Benerembah 2680
Benger 6223
Bengworden 3875
Benholme 4754
Benjaberring 6463
Benjinup 6255
Beni 2830
Bennetts Green 2290
Bennettswood 3125
Bennison 3960
Benowa 4217
Bensville 2251
Bentleigh 3204
Bentleigh East 3165
Bentley 2480
Bentley 6102
Bentley 6982
Bentley Park 4869
Berajondo 4674
Berala 2141
Beremboke 3342
Beresfield 2322
Berestford 6530
Bergalia 2537
Bergen 4353
Berkeley 2506
Berkeley Vale 2261
Berkshire Park 2765
Berkshire Valley 6510
Bermagui 2546
Bernier Island 6701
Berowra 2081

Berowra Heights 2082
Berowra Waters 2082
Berrambool 2548
Berrara 2540
Berri 5343
Berridale 2628
Berriedale 7011
Berrigan 2712
Berrilee 2159
Berrima 2577
Berrimah 0828
Berrimal 3518
Berrinba 4117
Berringa 3351
Berringama 3691
Berringer Lake 2539
Berriwillock 3531
Berry 2535
Berry Springs 0838
Berrybank 3323
Berrys Creek 3953
Berserker 4701
Bertram 6167
Berwick 3806
Bet Bet 3472
Bethanga 3691
Bethania 4205
Bethaney 5352
Bethungra 2590
Betley 3472
Beulah 3395
Beulah 7306
Beulah Park 5067
Beverford 3590
Beveridge 3753
Beverley 5009
Beverley 6304
Beverley Park 2217
Beverly Hills 2209

Bexhill 2480
Bexley 2207
Bibbenluke 2632
Bibra Lake 6163
Bicheno 7215
Bickley 6076
Bicton 6157
Biddelia 6260
Bidwill 2770
Big Grove 6330
Bigga 2583
Biggara 3707
Biggenden 4621
Diggers Waters 4216
Biggs Flat 5153
Bilambil 2486
Bilbarin 6375
Bilbul 2680
Bilgola 2107
Bilinga 4225
Bilingurr 6725
Billa Billa 4390
Billinudgel 2483
Biloela 4715
Bilpin 2758
Bimbi 2810
Bimbijy 6472
Bimbimbie 2536
Binalong 2584
Binalong Bay 7216
Binda 2583
Bindi Bindi 6574
Bindoon 6502
Binduli 6430
Bingara 2404
Bingegang 4702
Bingie 2537
Bingil Bay 4852
Binginwarri 3966

Binna Burra 2479
Binnaway 2395
Binningup 6233
Binnu 6532
Binnum 5262
Binya 2665
Birchgrove 2041
Birchip 3483
Birchmont 6214
Birchs Bay 7162
Birdsville 4482
Birdwood 5234
Birkdale 4159
Dirkenhead 5015
Birmingham Gardens
   2287
Birnnam 4352
Birralee 7303
Birregurra 3242
Birriwa 2844
Birrong 2143
Birtinya 4575
Bishops Bridge 2326
Bishopsbourne 7301
Bittern 3918
Black Duck Creek 4343
Black Forest 5035
Black Hill 2322
Black Hill 3350
Black Hill 5353
Black Hills 7140
Black Mountain 2365
Black Mountain 2601
Black River 4818
Black River 7321
Black Rock 3193
Black Snake 4600
Black Springs 2787
Black Swamp 2372

Blackall 4472
Blackalls Park 2283
Blackburn 3130
Blackbutt 2529
Blackbutt 4306
Blackdown 4702
Blackett 2770
Blackheath 2785
Blackmans Bay 7052
Blackmans Point 2444
Blacks Beach 4740
Blacksmiths 2281
Blacksoil 4306
Dlackstone 4304
Blacktown 2148
Blackville 2343
Blackwall 2256
Blackwall 2275
Blackwater 4717
Blackwood 3458
Blackwood 5051
Blackwood Creek 7301
Blair Athol 2560
Blair Athol 5084
Blairgowrie 3942
Blairmore 4625
Blairmount 2559
Blakehurst 2221
Blakeview 5114
Blakeville 3342
Blampied 3364
Blanchetown 5357
Blanchview 4352
Blandford 2338
Blanket Flat 2583
Blaxcell 2142
Blaxland 2774
Blaxlands Ridge 2758
Blayney 2799

Blessington 7212
Bli Bli 4560
Bligh Park 2756
Blighty 2713
Blind Bight 3980
Blinman 5730
Bloomsbury 4799
Blowhard 3352
Blue Bay 2261
Blue Haven 2262
Blue Mountain 4737
Blue Rocks 7255
Bluewater 4818
Bluff 4702
Bluff Point 6530
Blumont 7260
Blyth 5462
Blythdale 4455
Blythewood 6208
Boallia 6280
Boambee 2450
Boat Harbour 2316
Boat Harbour 7321
Bobalong 6320
Bobin 2429
Bobs Farm 2316
Bodalla 2545
Bodallin 6424
Bodangora 2820
Boddington 6390
Bogan 2825
Bogan Gate 2876
Bogangar 2488
Boggabilla 2409
Boggabri 2382
Bogie 4805
Bogong 3699
Bohle 4818

Bohle Plains 4817
Bohnock 2430
Boho South 3669
Boilup 6394
Boisdale 3860
Bokal 6392
Bokarina 4575
Bolgart 6568
Bolinda 3432
Bolivar 5110
Bolivia 2372
Bollier 4570
Bollon 4488
Dolong 2540
Bolton 3546
Bolton Point 2283
Bolwarra 2320
Bolwarra 3305
Bolwarrah 3352
Bomaderry 2541
Bombala 2632
Bombeeta 4871
Bombo 2533
Bon Accord 4625
Bonalbo 2469
Bonang 3888
Bonbeach 3196
Bond University 4229
Bondi 2026
Bondi Beach 2026
Bondi Junction 1355
Bondi Junction 2022
Bonegilla 3691
Bongaree 4507
Bongeen 4356
Bonnells Bay 2264
Bonnet Bay 2226
Bonnet Hill 7053
Bonnie Doon 3720

Bonnie Rock 6479
Bonny Hills 2445
Bonniefield 6525
Bonnyrigg 2177
Bonogin 4213
Bonshaw 2361
Bonshaw 4385
Bonville 2441
Bonython 2905
Booborowie 5417
Boodarie 6722
Boodarockin 6423
Boodua 4401
Boogan 4871
Booie 4610
Bookara 6525
Booker Bay 2257
Bookham 2582
Boolading 6392
Boolambayte 2423
Boolaroo 2284
Boolarra 3870
Boolboonda 4671
Booleroo Centre 5482
Booligal 2711
Boomi 2405
Boompa 4621
Boonah 4310
Boonanarring 6503
Boonara 4601
Boondall 4034
Boondandilla 4406
Boondooma 4613
Boonoo Boonoo 2372
Boonooroo 4650
Boorabbin 6429
Booragoon 6154
Booragoon 6954
Booragul 2284

Booral 2425
Booral 4655
Booralaming 6475
Boorara 6431
Boorcan 3265
Boorhaman 3678
Boorhaman North 3685
Booroorban 2710
Booroobin 4552
Boorowa 2586
Boort 3537
Bootenal 6532
Boothendarra 6521
Boouby Jan 4601
Booval 4304
Booyal 4671
Borallon 4306
Borambil 2329
Boranup 6286
Borden 6338
Borderdale 6320
Bordertown 5268
Boree Creek 2652
Boreen Point 4565
Borenore 2800
Bornholm 6330
Boro 2622
Boronia 3155
Boronia Heights 4124
Bororen 4678
Borroloola 0854
Borung 3518
Boscabel 6394
Bossley Park 2176
Bostobrick 2453
Botany 1455
Botany 2019
Bothwell 7030
Boulder 6432

Boulder Creek 4714
Bouldercombe 4702
Boulia 4829
Boundain 6312
Boundary Bend 3599
Bourke 2840
Bournda 2550
Bouvard 6210
Bovell 6280
Bow Bowing 2566
Bow Bridge 6333
Bowden 5007
Bowelling 6225
Bowen 4805
Bowen Hills 4006
Bowen Mountain 2753
Bowenfels 2790
Bowenville 4404
Bower 5374
Bowes 6535
Bowgada 6623
Bowhill 5238
Bowling Alley Point 2340
Bowmans 5550
Bowmans Forest 3735
Bowna 2644
Bowning 2582
Bowral 2576
Bowraville 2449
Box Hill 2765
Box Hill 3128
Box Hill North 3129
Box Hill South 2128
Boxwood 3725
Boxwood Hill 6338
Boya 6056
Boyanup 6237
Boyatup 6450
Boyer 7140

Boyerine 6316
Boyne Island 4680
Boyne Valley 4680
Boynedale 6810
Boyneside 4610
Boynewood 4626
Boyup Brook 6244
Bracalba 4512
Bracewell 4695
Bracken Ridge 4017
Bracknell 7302
Bradbury 2560
Bradbury 5153
Braddon 2612
Bradys Lake 7140
Braemar 2628
Braemore 4313
Braeside 3195
Brahma Lodge 5109
Braidwood 2622
Bramley 6285
Brampton Island 4741
Branch Creek 4625
Branchview 4352
Branditt 3630
Brandon 4808
Brandy Creek 4800
Brandy Hill 2324
Branxholm 7261
Branxholme 3302
Branxton 2335
Branyan 4670
Brassall 4305
Bray Park 2484
Bray Park 4500
Braybrook 3019
Brazier 6251
Breadalbane 2581
Breadalbane 4800

Breadalbane 7258
Breakaway 4825
Breakwater 3219
Bream Creek 7175
Breamlea 3227
Bredbo 2626
Breera 6503
Breeza 2381
Bremer 4305
Bremer Bay 6338
Brendale 4500
Brentford Square 3131
Brentwood 5575
Brentwood 6153
Breona 7304
Breton Bay 6043
Bretti 2422
Brewarrina 2839
Brewongle 2795
Briagolong 3860
Briar Hill 3088
Bribbaree 2594
Bribie Island 4507
Bridgeman Downs 4035
Bridgenorth 7277
Bridgetown 6255
Bridgewater 5155
Bridgewater 7030
Bridgewater On Loddon 3516
Bridport 7262
Brigadoon 6056
Brigalow 4412
Bright 3741
Brighton 3186
Brighton 4017
Brighton 5048
Brighton 7030
Brighton East 3187

Brighton-Le-Sands 2216
Brightwaters 2264
Brim 3391
Brindabella 2611
Bringalily 4357
Bringelly 2171
Brengenbrong 3707
Bringo 6532
Brinkin 0810
Brinkworth 5464
Brinsmead 4870
Brisbane Adelaide Street 4000
Brisbane City 4000
Brisbane private boxes 4001
Brisbane Market 4106
Brittons Swamp 7330
Broadbeach 4218
Broadford 3658
Broadmarsh 7030
Broadmeadow 2292
Broadmeadows 3047
Broadmere 4420
Broadview 5083
Broadwater 2472
Broadwater 2549
Broadwater 3301
Broadwater 6380
Broadway 2007
Broadway Nedlands 6009
Broadwood 6430
Brocklehurst 2830
Brocklesby 2642
Brockman 6701
Brogo 2550
Broke 2330
Broke 6398

Broken Head 2481
Broken Hill 2880
Broken River 4757
Brompton 5007
Bronte 2024
Bronte Park 7140
Brookdale 6112
Brookfield 3338
Brookfield 4069
Brookhampton 6239
Brookhill 4816
Brooklet 2479
Brooklyn 2083
Brooklyn 3012
Brooklyn 7320
Brooklyn Park 5032
Brookside Centre 4053
Brookstead 4364
Brookton 6306
Brookvale 2100
Brookwater 4300
Broome 6725
Broomehill 6318
Broomfield 3364
Brooms Head 2463
Brooweena 4620
Broulee 2537
Brovinia 4626
Brown Hill 3350
Brown Hill 6431
Brownhill Creek 5062
Browns Range 6701
Browns Creek 2799
Browns Plains 3685
Browns Plains 4118
Brownsville 2530
Broxburn 4356
Bruce 2617
Bruce Rock 6418

Brukunga 5252
Brundee 2540
Brungle 2722
Brunkerville 2323
Brunswick 3056
Brunswick 6224
Brunswick East 3057
Brunswick Heads 2483
Brunswick West 3055
Brush Creek 4387
Brushgrove 2460
Bruthen 3885
Bryden 4312
Brymaroo 4403
Buangor 3375
Buaraba South 4311
Bucasia 4750
Buccan 4207
Buchan 3885
Buchfelde 5118
Buckenbowra 2536
Buckingham 4825
Buckingham 6225
Buckland 6401
Buckland 7190
Buckland Park 5120
Buckleboo 5641
Buckley 3240
Budderoo 2535
Buddina 4575
Buderim 4556
Budgee 4359
Budgewoi 2262
Buff Point 2262
Buffalo 3958
Buffalo River 3737
Bugaldie 2357
Bugle Ranges 5251
Builyan 4680

Bukali 4630
Bukkulla 2360
Bulandelah 2423
Bulga 2330
Bulgarra 6714
Bulimba 4171
Bull creek 6149
Bulla 3428
Bullabulling 6429
Bullaburra 2784
Bullaring 6373
Bullarook 3352
Bullarto 3461
Bullcamp 4615
Bulleen 3105
Bullengarook 3437
Buller 6353
Bullfinch 6484
Bulli 2516
Bulli Creek 4357
Bullock Hills 6317
Bullsbrook 6084
Buln Buln 3821
Bulong 6431
Bulwer 4025
Bulyee 6306
Bumbaldry 2794
Bunbartha 3634
Bunbury 6230
Bunbury 6231
Bundabah 2324
Bundaberg 4670
Bundalaguah 3851
Bundall 4217
Bundalong 3730
Bundamba 4304
Bundanoon 2578
Bundanoon 6522
Bundarra 2359

Bundeena 2230
Bundook 2422
Bundoora 3083
Bungador 3260
Bungalow 4870
Bungarby 2630
Bungaree 3352
Bungeet 3726
Bungendore 2621
Bungeworgorai 4455
Bungil 4455
Bungonia 2580
Bungulla 2372
Bungulla 6410
Bungunya 4494
Bungwahl 2423
Buniche 6353
Buninyong 3357
Bunjil 6623
Bunnaloo 2731
Bunnan 2337
Buntine 6613
Bunya 4055
Bunya Creek 4655
Bunya Mountains 4405
Bunyah 2429
Bunyan 2630
Bunyip 3815
Burakin 6467
Buraminya 6452
Buranda 4102
Burbank 4156
Burcher 2671
Burekup 6227
Burges 6302
Burgooney 2672
Burgown 4659
Burketown 4830
Burleigh 4822

Burleigh Heads 4220
Burlong 6401
Burnett Heads 4670
Burnie 7320
Burnley 3121
Burns Beach 6028
Burns Creek 7212
Burnside 3023
Burnside 5066
Burnside 6285
Buronga 2739
Burpengary 4505
Burra 2620
Burra 5417
Burracoppin 6421
Burradoo 2576
Burraga 2795
Burragate 2550
Burran Rock 6490
Burrawang 2577
Burrell Creek 2429
Burren Junction 2386
Burrier 2540
Burrill Lake 2539
Burringbar 2483
Burrinjuck 2582
Burrowye 3709
Burrum Heads 4659
Burrumbeet 3352
Burrumbuttock 2642
Burrup 6714
Burswood 6100
Burton 4742
Burton 5110
Burwood 1805
Burwood 2134
Burwood 3125
Burwood East 3151
Burwood Heights 2136

Burwood Heights 3151
Busby 2168
Bushfield 3281
Bushland Beach 4818
Bushley 4702
Bushy Park 7140
Busselton 6280
Butchers Ridge 3885
Bute 5560
Buttler 5605
Butler 6036
Butlers Gorge 7140
Buttaba 2283
Buxton 2571
Buxton 3711
Buxton 4660
Byabarra 2446
Byaduk 3301
Bybera 4387
Byellee 4680
Byfield 4703
Byford 6122
Bygalorie 2669
Bylands 3762
Bylong 2849
Bymount 4455
Byrneside 3617
Byrock 2831
Byron Bay 2481

C

Cabarita 2137
Cabarita 3505
Cabarita Beach 2488
Cabarlah 4352
Cabbage Tree Creek
    3889
Cabbage Tree Island
    2477

Cable Beach 6726
Caboolture 4510
Caboonbah 4312
Cabramatta 2166
Cabramurra 2629
Cadell 5321
Cadoux 6466
Caffey 4343
Caiguna 6443
Cairnlea 3023
Cairns 4870
Cairns Bay 7116
Carins North 4870
Cal Lal 2648
Calala 2340
Calamvale 4116
Calavos 4670
Calca 5671
Calder 7325
Caldermeade 3984
Caldervale 4478
Caldwell 2710
Calen 4798
Calga 2250
Calgoa 4570
California Gully 3556
Calingiri 6569
Calingunee 4390
Calista 6167
Calivil 3573
Caljie 6302
Callaghan 2308
Callala Bay 2540
Callala Beach 2540
Callandoon 4390
Callemondah 4680
Callide 4715
Callignee 3844
Callington 5254

Calliope 4680
Caloundra 4551
Caltowie 5490
Calulu 3875
Calwell 2905
Camberwell 2330
Camberwell 3124
Camberwell East 3126
Cambewarra 2540
Camboon 4719
Cambooya 4358
Cambrai 5353
Cambrian Hill 3352
Cambridge 7170
Cambridge Gulf 6743
Cambridge Park 2747
Cambroon 4552
Camden 2570
Camden Head 2443
Camden Park 2570
Camden Park 5038
Camellia 2142
Camena 7316
Camira 4300
Cammeray 2062
Camoola 4730
Camooweal 4828
Camp Creek 4871
Camp Hill 4152
Camp Mountain 4520
Campania 7026
Campbell 2612
Campbell Creek 4625
Campbell Town 7210
Campbellfield 3061
Campbells Bridge 3381
Campbells Creek 3451
Campbells Forest 3556
Campbelltown 2560

Campbelltown 3364
Campbelltown 5074
Camperdown 1450
Camperdown 2050
Camperdown 3260
Campsie 2194
Campvale 2318
Campwin Beach 4737
Cams Wharf 2281
Canada Bay 2046
Canadian 3350
Canal Creek 4702
Canary Island 3537
Canberra City 2600
Canberra private boxes
    2601
Cancanning 6315
Candelo 2550
Cane 6710
Cangai 2460
Cania 4630
Caniambo 3630
Canina 4570
Canley Heights 2166
Canley Vale 2166
Cann River 3890
Canna 6627
Cannie 3540
Cannindah 4630
Canning Bridge
    Applecross 6153
Canning Creek 4357
Canning Mills 6111
Canning Vale 6155
Cannington 6107
Cannington 6987
Cannon Hill 4170
Cannons Creek 3977
Cannonvale 4802

Canonba 2825
Canoona 4702
Canowindra 2804
Canterbury 2193
Canterbury 3126
Canungra 4275
Capalaba 4157
Caparra 2429
Cape Arid 6452
Cape Barren Island 7257
Cape Burney 6532
Cape Clear 3351
Cape Conway 4800
Cape Gloucester 4800
Cape Hillsborough 4740
Cape le Grand 6450
Cape Moreton 4025
Cape Paterson 3995
Cape Portland 7264
Cape Range National
   Park 6707
Cape Woolamai 3925
Capel 6271
Capella 4732
Capertee 2846
Capricorn 6642
Captain Creek 4677
Captains Flat 2623
Captains Mountain 4357
Caraban 6041
Carabooda 6033
Carabost 2650
Caragabal 2810
Caramut 3274
Carani 6566
Carapook 3312
Caravonica 4878
Carbrook 4130
Carbunup River 6280

Carcoar 2791
Cardiff 6225
Cardiff 2285
Cardigan 3352
Cardinia 3978
Cardross 3496
Cardstone 4854
Cardup 6122
Cardwell 4849
Careel Bay 2107
Carey Bay 2283
Carey Gully 5144
Carey Park 6230
Cargo 2800
Carina 4152
Carinda 2831
Carindale 4152
Carine 6020
Caringbah 1495
Caringbah 2229
Carisbrook 3464
Carlingford 2118
Carlisle 6101
Carlisle River 3239
Carlotta 6275
Carlsruhe 3442
Carlton 2218
Carlton 3053
Carlton 7173
Carlton North 3054
Carlton South 3053
Carmel 6076
Carmila 4739
Carnamah 6517
Carnarvon 6701
Carnegie 3163
Carngham 3351
Carole Park 4300
Caroline Springs 3023

Carool 2486
Caroona 2343
Carpendale 4344
Carpenter Rocks 5291
Carrabin 6423
Carrai 2440
Carrajung 3844
Carrajung South 3874
Carramar 2163
Carramar 6031
Carranballac 3361
Carrandotta 4825
Carrara 4211
Carrathool 2711
Carrick 7291
Carrickalinga 5204
Carrieton 5432
Carrington 2294
Carrington 2324
Carrington 4883
Carroll 2340
Carrolup 6317
Carrowbrook 2330
Carrum 3197
Carrum Downs 3201
Carseldine 4034
Carss Park 2221
Carstairs 4806
Cartmeticup 6316
Cartwright 2168
Carwarp 3494
Cascade 6450
Casey 7150
Cashmere 4500
Casino 2470
Cassilis 2329
Castambul 5076
Castaways Beach 4567
Casterton 3311

Castle Cove 2069
Castle Creek 4715
Castle Forbes Bay 7116
Castle Hill 1765
Castle Hill 2154
Castle Hill 4810
Castlecrag 2068
Castlemaine 3450
Castlereagh 2749
Castletown 6450
Casuarina 0810
Casuarina 6167
Casuarina private boxes
   0811
Casula 2170
Cataby 6507
Catalina 2536
Catani 3981
Cathcart 2632
Catherine Field 2557
Catherine Hill Bay 2281
Cathkin 3714
Cattai 2756
Catterick 6255
Cattle Creek 4407
Cattle Creek 4626
Caulfield 3162
Caulfield East 3145
Caulfield North 3161
Caulfield South 3162
Causeway 2604
Causeway Lake 4703
Cavan 5094
Cavendish 3314
Caversham 6055
Caves Beach 2281
Caveside 7304
Cawdor 2570
Cawongla 2474

Cecil Hills 2171
Cecil Park 2171
Cecil Plains 4407
Cedar Creek 4207
Cedar Creek 4520
Cedar Grove 4285
Cedar Vale 4285
Ceduna 5690
Cells River 2324
Cement Mills 4352
Centenary Heights 4350
Centennial Park 2021
Centennial Park 6330
Central Macdonald 2775
Central Park 3145
Central Plaza 4001
Central Queensland
   University 4701
Central Tilba 2546
Ceratodus 4627
Ceres 3221
Cervantes 6511
Cessnock 2325
Chadstone 3148
Chadwick 6450
Chahpingah 4610
Chain Of Lagoons 7215
Chain Valley Bay 2259
Chakola 2630
Chambers Flat 4133
Champion Lakes 6111
Chandler 4155
Chandler 6490
Chandlers Hill 5159
Changerup 6394
Chapel Hill 4069
Chapman 2611
Chapman Hill 6280
Chapple Vale 3239

Charbon 2848
Charleroi 3695
Charles Darwin
University 0815
Charles Darwin
University 0909
Charles Sturt University
2678
Charleston 5244
Charlestown 2290
Charlestown 4608
Charleville 4470
Charley Creek 6239
Charlotte Bay 2428
Charlton 3525
Charmhaven 2263
Charnwood 2615
Charters Towers 4820
Chatham 2430
Chatswood 2057
Chatswood 2067
Chatsworth 2759
Chatsworth 3379
Cheepie 4475
Chelmer 4068
Chelmsford 4606
Chelsea 3196
Chelsea Heights 3196
Cheltenham 2119
Cheltenham 3192
Cheltenham 4627
Cheltenham 5014
Chepstowe 3351
Cherbourg 4605
Chermside 4032
Cherry Creek 4306
Cherry Gardens 5157
Cherry Tree Pool 6395
Cherrybrook 2126

Cherryville 5134
Cherwell 4660
Cheshunt 3678
Chester Hill 2162
Chetwynd 3312
Chevron Island 4217
Chewton 3451
Cheynes 6328
Chichester 6751
Chidlow 6556
Chifley 2036
Chifley 2606
Chigwell 7011
Childers 3824
Childers 4660
Chillagoe 4871
Chillingham 2484
Chiltern 3683
Chinchilla 4413
Chinderah 2487
Chinkapook 3546
Chippendale 2008
Chipping Norton 2170
Chirn Park 4215
Chirnside Park 3116
Chisholm 2905
Chiswick 2046
Chittaway Bay 2261
Chittaway Point 2259
Chittering 6084
Chorregon 4730
Chowerup 6244
Christie Downs 5164
Christies Beach 5165
Christmas Hills 3775
Christmas Hills 7330
Christmas Island 6798
Chudleigh 7304
Chullora 2190

Church Point 2105
Churchable 4311
Churchill 3842
Churchill 4305
Churchlands 6018
Chuwar 4306
City 2601
City Beach 6015
City East 4002
Civic Square 2608
Clackline 6564
Clagiraba 4211
Clandulla 2848
Clapham 5062
Clare 4807
Clare 5453
Claremont 6010
Claremont 6910
Claremont 7011
Clarence 2790
Clarence Gardens 5039
Clarence Park 5034
Clarence Point 7270
Clarence Town 2321
Clarendon 2756
Clarendon 3357
Clarendon 5157
Clarendon Vale 7019
Clarinda 3169
Clarke Creek 4705
Clarkefield 3430
Clarkes Hill 3352
Clarkson 6030
Claude Road 7306
Claverton 4471
Clayfield 4011
Claymore 2559
Clayton 3168
Clayton 5256

Clayton South 3169
Clear Island Waters 4226
Clear Mountain 4500
Clearview 5085
Cleary 6472
Cleaverville 6714
Clematis 3782
Clemton Park 2206
Clermont 4721
Cleve 5640
Cleveland 4163
Cleveland 7211
Clifton 2515
Clifton 4361
Clifton 6210
Clifton Beach 4879
Clifton Beach 7020
Clifton Hill 3068
Clifton Springs 3222
Clinton 4680
Clinton 5570
Cloisters Square
Clonbinane 3658
Cloncurry 4824
Clontarf 2093
Clontarf 4019
Clontarf 4357
Closeburn 4520
Clovelly 2031
Clovelly Park 5042
Clovelly West 2031
Cloverdale 6105
Cloverdale 6985
Cloyna 4605
Club Terrace 3889
Cluden 4811
Clunes 2480
Clunes 3370
Clybucca 2440

Clyde 3978
Coal Point 2283
Coalcliff 2508
Coaldale 2460
Coalfalls 4305
Coalville 3825
Coatesville 3165
Cobar 2835
Cobar Park 2790
Cobargo 2550
Cobbadah 2347
Cobbitty 2570
Cobbora 2844
Cobbs Hill 4605
Cobden 3266
Cobdogla 5346
Coblinine 6317
Cobraball 4703
Cobram 3644
Cobram private boxes
3643
Coburg 3058
Cockatoo 3781
Cockatoo 4419
Cockatoo Valley 5351
Cockburn 5440
Cocklebiddy 6443
Coconut Grove 0810
Coconuts 4860
Codjatotine 6308
Coen 4871
Coffin Bay 5607
Coffs Harbour 2450
Coghills Creek 3364
Cohuna 3568
Coila 2537
Coimadai 3337
Colac 3250
Colac Colac 3707

Corinda 4075
Corindhap 3352
Corindi Beach 2456
Corinella 3984
Coringa 4621
Corinthia 6426
Corio 3214
Corlette 2315
Corndale 2480
Corndale 4610
Cornubia 4130
Cornwall 4455
Cornwall 7215
Cornwallis 2756
Corny Point 5575
Corobimilla 2700
Coromandel East 5157
Coromandel Valley 5051
Coronet Bay 3984
Corop 3559
Cororooke 3254
Corowa 2646
Corrigin 6375
Corrimal 2518
Corryong 3707
Corunnun 3249
Cosgrove 3631
Cosmo Newberry 6440
Cossack 6720
Costerfield 3523
Cottesloe 6011
Cottesloe 6911
Cottles Bridge 3099
Cotton Tree 4558
Cottonvale 4375
Coulta 5607
Couridjah 2571
Courtenay 6288
Coutts Crossing 2460

Coverty 4613
Cowalellup 6336
Cowalla 6503
Cowan 2081
Cowan Cowan 4025
Cowandilla 5033
Cowangie 3506
Cowaramup 6284
Cowcowing 6485
Cowell 5602
Cowes 3922
Cowley 4871
Cowper 2460
Cowra 2794
Cowwarr 3857
Coyrecup 6317
Crabbes Creek 2483
Crabtree 7109
Crace 2911
Cradle Mountain 7306
Cradoc 7109
Cradock 5432
Crafers 5152
Craigburn Farm 5051
Craigie 2632
Craigie 3465
Craigie 6025
Craigieburn 3064
Craigmore 5114
Cramphorne 6420
Cranbourne 3977
Cranbrook 4814
Cranbrook 6321
Cranbrook 7190
Cranebrook 2749
Cranley 4350
Craven 2422
Crawley 6009
Crediton 4757

Creek Junction 3669
Creighton 3666
Cremorne 2090
Cremorne 3121
Cremorne 7024
Cremorne Junction 2090
Crescent Head 2440
Cressy 3322
Cressy 7302
Crestmead 4132
Crestwood 2620
Creswick 3363
Crib Point 3919
Cringila 2502
Crohamhurst 4519
Croker Island 0822
Cromarty 4809
Cromer 2099
Cromer 3193
Cronulla 2230
Crooble 2400
Crooked Brook 6236
Crooked Corner 2583
Crookwell 2583
Croppa Creek 2411
Crossdale 4312
Cross Roads 5558
Crossman 6390
Croudace Bay 2280
Crowdy Head 2427
Crowea 6258
Crowlands 3377
Crows Nest 1585
Crows Nest 2065
Crows Nest 4355
Crowther 2803
Croydon 2132
Croydon 3136
Croydon 4871

Croydon 5008
Croydon Park 2133
Cryon 2832
Crystal Brook 4800
Crystal Brook 5523
Crystal Creek 2484
Cuballing 6311
Cubbine 6383
Cudal 2864
Cudgee 3265
Cudgen 2487
Cudgera Creek 2484
Cudgewa 3705
Cudlee Creek 5232
Cudmirrah 2540
Cue 6640
Culburra 5261
Culburra Beach 2540
Culcairn 2660
Culgoa 3530
Culham 6566
Cullacabardee 6067
Cullalla 6503
Cullen Bullen 2790
Cullinane 4860
Cullulleraine 3496
Cumberland Park 5041
Cumborah 2832
Cummins 5631
Cumnock 2867
Cundare North 3251
Cundeelee 6434
Cunderdin 6407
Cundinup 6275
Cundle Flat 2424
Cundletown 2430
Cungena 5660
Cungulla 4816
Cunjardine 6401

Cunjurong Point 2539
Cunnamulla 4490
Cuprona 7316
Curban 2827
Curdievale 3268
Curdies River 3268
Curl Curl 2096
Curlewis 2381
Curlewis 3222
Curlwaa 2648
Curra 4570
Currabubula 2342
Currajah 4871
Currajong 4812
Currambine 6028
Curramore 4552
Curramulka 5580
Currans Hill 2567
Currarong 2540
Currency Creek 5214
Currie 7256
Currimundi 4551
Currowan 2536
Currumbin 4223
Curtin 2605
Cutella 4352
Cuthbert 6330
Cuttabri 2388
Cuttaburra 4490
Cuttagee 2546
Cygnet 7112
Cynthia 4627
Cypress Gardens 4357

D

Daadenning Creek 6410
Daceyville 2032
Dadswells Bridge 3385
Daggar Hills 6638

Daglish 6008
D'aguilar 4514
Daintree 4873
Dairy Plains 7304
Daisy Hill 4127
Daisy Hill 3465
Dajarra 4825
Dakabin 4503
Dakenba 4715
Dalbeg 4807
Dalby 4405
Dale 6304
Daleys Point 2257
Dalgety 2628
Daliak 6302
Dalkeith 6009
Dallas 3047
Dalma 4702
Dalmeny 2546
Dalmore 3981
Dalrymple Heights 4757
Dalton 2581
Dalveen 4374
Dalwallinu 6609
Dalwood 2335
Dalwood 2477
Daly River 0822
Daly Waters 0852
Dalyellup 6230
Dalysford 4671
Dalyston 3992
Dalyup 6450
Damascus 4671
Dampier 6713
Dampier Archipelago
    6713
Dampier Peninsula 6725
Danbulla 4872
Dandanning 6479

Dandaragan 6507
Dandenong 3175
Dandenong South
    private boxes 3164
Dandongadale 3737
Dangar 2309
Dangar Island 2083
Dangin 6383
Dangore 4610
Dapto 2530
Daradgee 4860
Darbys Falls 2793
Darch 6065
Dardanup 6236
Dareton 2717
Dargan 2786
Dargo 3862
Dark Corner 2795
Darkan 6392
Darke Peak 5642
Darkes Forest 2508
Darlimurla 3871
Darling 3145
Darling Downs 6122
Darling Heights 4350
Darling Point 2027
Darlinghurst 1300
Darlinghurst 2010
Darlington 2008
Darlington 3271
Darlington 5047
Darlington 6070
Darlington Point 2706
Darnum 3822
Daroobalgie 2870
Darra 4076
Darradup 6275
Darraweit Guim 3756
Darriman 3851

Dartbrook 2336
Dartmoor 3304
Dartmoor 6532
Dartmouth 3701
Dartnall 6320
Darts Creek 4695
Darwin City 0800
Darwin GPO private
    boxes 0801
Darwin Mail Centre 0822
Datatie 6317
Davenport 6230
Daveson 4855
Davidson 2085
Davis 7151
Davis Creek 2336
Davistown 2251
Davoren Park 5113
Daw Park 5041
Dawes Point 2000
Dawesville 6210
Dayboro 4521
Daydream Island 4741
Daylesford 3460
Daymar 4497
Daysdale 2646
De Grey 6722
Deagon 4017
Deakin 2600
Deakin University 3217
Dean 3352
Dean Park 2761
Deanmill 6258
Deans Marsh 3235
Deception Bay 4508
Deddington 7212
Dederang 3691
Dee 7140
Dee Why 2099

Deebing Heights 4306
Deep Bay 7112
Deep Creek 4625
Deepdale 6532
Deepdene 6290
Deepwater 2371
Deepwater 4674
Deer Park 3023
Deer Park East 3022
Deeragun 4818
Deeral 4871
Degilbo 4621
Delacombe 3356
Delahey 3037
Delamere 5204
Delan 4671
Delegate 2633
Delissaville 0822
Deloraine 7304
Delungra 2403
Denbarker 6324
Dendy 3186
Denham 6537
Denham Court 2565
Denhams Beach 2536
Deniliquin 2710
Denistone 2114
Denistone East 2112
Denman 2328
Denmark 6333
Dennes Point 7150
Dennington 3280
Derby 3516
Derby 6728
Derby 7264
Dereel 3352
Dergholm 3312
Dernancourt 5075
Derri Derra 4626

Derrimut 3030
Derrinallum 3325
Derriwong 2877
Derrymore 4352
Derwent Bridge 7140
Derwent Park 7009
Deua 2537
Deua River Valley 2537
Deuchar 4362
Devenish 3726
Devereux Creek 4753
Devils Creek 6630
Deviot 7275
Devon Hills 7300
Devon Meadows 3977
Devon North 3971
Devon Park 4401
Devon Park 5008
Devonport 7310
Dewars Pool 6567
Dharruk 2770
Dharug 3610
Diamantina Lakes 4735
Diamond Beach 2430
Diamond Creek 3089
Diamond Tree 6258
Diamond Valley 4553
Dianella 6062
Dickson 2602
Dicky Beach 4551
Didcot 4621
Diddillibah 4559
Digby 3309
Diggers Rest 3427
Diglum 4680
Dignams Creek 2546
Dilston 7252
Dimboola 3414
Dimbulah 4872

Dindiloa 6532
Dingee 3571
Dingley Village 3172
Dingo 4702
Dingup 6258
Dinmore 4303
Dinner Plain 3898
Dinninup 6244
Dinoga 2404
Direk 5110
Dirnbir 4625
Dirranbandi 4486
Dittmer 4800
Diwan 4873
Dixalea 4702
Dixons Creek 3775
Dixvale 6258
Djiru 4852
Djuan 4352
Djugun 6725
Dobies Bight 2470
Docklands 3008
Doctor Creek 4352
Doctor George Mountain 2550
Doctors Rocks 7325
Dodges Ferry 7173
Dog Swamp 6060
Dolans Bay 2229
Don 7310
Domville 4357
Don 7310
Donald 3480
Doncaster 3108
Doncaster East 3109
Doncaster Heights 3109
Dongara 6525
Dongolocking 6315
Donnelly River 6255

Donnybrook 3064
Donnybrook 4510
Donnybrook 6239
Donovans 5291
Donvale 3111
Doodenanning 6383
Doodlakine 6411
Dooen 3401
Dookie 3646
Dookie College 3647
Doolandella 4077
Doomadgee 4830
Doon Doon 2484
Doongin 6409
Doongul 4620
Doonside 2767
Dooralong 2259
Dora Creek 2264
Doreen 3754
Dorre Island 6701
Dorrigo 2453
Dorrington 4060
Dorroughby 2480
Double Bay 1360
Double Bay 2028
Doubleview 6018
Doubtful Creek 2470
Doughboy 4671
Douglas 3409
Douglas 4354
Douglas 4814
Douglas Park 2569
Douglas River 7215
Dover 7117
Dover Gardens 5048
Dover Heights 2030
Doveton 3177
Dowerin 6461
Downer 2602

Downsfield 4570
Downside 2650
Dows Creek 4754
Dowsing Poing 7010
Doyalson 2262
Draper 4520
Drayton 4350
Dreeite 3249
Drewvale 4116
Drillham 4424
Drinan 4671
Dripstone 2820
Driver 0830
Dromana 3936
Drome 6330
Dromedary 4718
Dromedary 7030
Drouin 3818
Drummond 3461
Drummond North 3446
Drummond Cove 6532
Drummoyne 1470
Drummoyne 2047
Dry Creek 5094
Dryandra 6311
Drysdale 3222
Drysdale River 6740
Duaringa 4712
Dubbo 2830
Dublin 5501
Duckinwilla 4650
Duckmaloi 2787
Dudawa 6519
Dudinin 6363
Dudley 2290
Dudley Park 5008
Dudley Park 6210
Duffys Forest 2084
Duffy 2611

Duingal 4671
Dukin 6475
Dulacca 4425
Dulbelling 6383
Dulcot 7025
Dulong 4560
Dululu 4702
Dulwich 5065
Dulwich Hill 2203
Dulyalbin 6425
Dumbalk 3956
Dumbarton 6566
Dumberning 6312
Dumbleyung 6350
Dumgree 4715
Dumpy Creek 4702
Dunalley 7177
Dunbible 2484
Dunbogan 2443
Duncraig 6023
Dundarrah 4625
Dundas 2117
Dundas 6443
Dundathu 4650
Dundee 2370
Dundee Beach 0840
Dundonnell 3271
Dundowran Beach 4655
Dundula 4740
Dundurrabin 2453
Dunedoo 2844
Dungay 2484
Dungog 2420
Dungowan 2340
Dunkeld 2795
Dunkeld 3294
Dunkirk 3630
Dunlop 2615
Dunmora 4650

Dunmore 2529
Dunmore 4407
Dunn Rock 6355
Dunnrock 4740
Dunnstown 3352
Dunolly 3472
Dunoon 2480
Dunorlan 7304
Dunsborough 6281
Duntroon 2600
Dunwich 4183
Durack 4077
Durack 6743
Dural 2158
Dural 2330
Duramana 2795
Duranbah 2487
Duranillin 6393
Durawah 6532
Durham Downs 4454
Durham Lead 3352
Durham Ox 3576
Duri 2344
Durong 4610
Durras North 2536
Durren Durren 2259
Dutton Park 4102
Duverney 3323
Dwarda 6308
Dwellingup 6213
Dyers Crossing 2429
Dykehead 4626
Dynnyrne 7005
Dyraaba 2470
Dysart 4745
Dysart 7030

Emita 7255
Emmaville 2371
Empire Bay 2257
Empire Vale 2478
Emu 3475
Emu Flat 6431
Emu Park 4702
Emu Plains 2750
Emu Point 6330
Emu Vale 4371
Encounter Bay 5211
Endeavour Hills 3802
Eneabba 6518
Enfield 2136
Enfield 3352
Enfield 5085
Enfield South 2133
Engadine 2233
Englorie Park 2560
Enmore 2042
Enmore 2350
Enmore 2358
Enngonia 2840
Ennuin 6484
Enoggera 4051
Enoggera Reservoir 4052
Ensay 3895
Eppalock 3551
Epping 1710
Epping 2121
Epping 3076
Epping Forest 7211
Epsom 3551
Epsom 4741
Eradu 6532
Erakala 4740
Eraring 2264
Erica 3825
Erigolia 2669

Erina 2250
Erindale 5066
Erindale Centre 2903
Ermington 1700
Ermington 2115
Ernabella 0872
Ernestina 4730
Eromanga 4480
Erowal Bay 2540
Erriba 7310
Erskine 6210
Erskine Park 2759
Erskineville 2043
Eschol Park 2558
Esk 4312
Eskdale 3701
Esperance 6450
Essendon 3040
Essendon North 3041
Ethelton 5015
Etmilyn 6213
Etna Creek 4702
Eton 4741
Ettalong Beach 2257
Ettrick 2474
Etty Bay 4858
Euabalong 2877
Eubenangee 4860
Euchareena 2866
Eucla 6443
Eucumbene 2628
Eudlo 4554
Eudunda 5374
Eugenana 7310
Eugowra 2806
Euleilah 4674
Eulo 4491
Eumamurrin 4455
Eumundi 4562

Eumungerie 2831
Eungai Creek 2441
Eungella 2484
Eungella 4757
Eungella Hinterland 4741
Euramo 4854
Eurardy 6532
Eureka 2480
Eureka 3350
Eureka 4660
Eurimbula 4677
Euroa 3666
Eurobin 3739
Eurong 4581
Euston 2737
Euthulla 4455
Evandale 5069
Evandale 7212
Evans Head 2473
Evans Landing 4874
Evansford 3371
Evanslea 4356
Evanston 5116
Evatt 2617
Eveleigh 2015
Evelyn 4888
Everard Park 5035
Evergreen 4352
Everton 3678
Everton Hills 4053
Everton Park 4053
Ewlyamartup 6317
Exeter 2579
Exeter 5019
Exeter 7275
Exford 3338
Exmouth 6707
Export Park 5950
Exton 7303

F
Fadden 2904
Failford 2430
Fairbridge 6208
Fairdale 4606
Fairfield 1860
Fairfield 2165
Fairfield 3078
Fairfield 4103
Fairhaven 3231
Fairlight 2094
Fairney View 4306
Fairview Park 5126
Fairy Bower 4700
Fairy Hill 2470
Fairy Meadow 2519
Falcon 6210
Falls Creek 2540
Falls Creek 3699
Falmouth 7215
Fannie Bay 0820
Farleigh 4741
Farley 2320
Farmborough Heights 2526
Farnham 2820
Farrar 0830
Farrell Flat 5416
Farrer 2607
Fassifern 2283
Faulconbridge 2776
Fawkner 3060
Federal 2480
Federal 4568
Felixstow 5070
Felton 4358
Fennell Bay 2283
Fentonbury 7140
Ferguson 6236

Fern Bay 2295
Fern Hill 3458
Fern Tree 7054
Fernbank 3864
Ferndale 6148
Ferney 4650
Fernihurst 3518
Fernleigh 2479
Fernmount 2454
Ferntree Gully 3156
Fernvale 4306
Ferny Creek 3786
Ferny Grove 4055
Ferny Hills 4055
Ferryden Park 5010
Feysville 6431
Fiddletown 2159
Fifield 2875
Fifteen Mile 4352
Fig Tree Pocket 4069
Figtree 2525
Fimiston 6432
Finch Hatton 4756
Findon 5023
Fingal 3939
Fingal 7214
Fingal Bay 2315
Fingal Head 2487
Finke 0872
Finley 2713
Finnie 4350
Finniss 5255
Finucane 6722
Firefly 2429
Firle 5070
Fish Creek 3959
Fisher 2611
Fisher 4825
Fishermans Pocket 4570

Fishery Falls 4871
Fishing Point 2283
Fitzgerald 6337
Fitzgerald 7140
Fitzgerald Creek 4860
Fitzgibbon 4018
Fitzroy 3065
Fitzroy 5082
Fitzroy Crossing 6765
Fitzroy Falls 2577
Fitzroy North 3068
Five Dock 2046
Five Ways 3977
Flagstaff Hill 5159
Flagstone Creek 4344
Flametree 4802
Flaxley 5153
Flemington 3031
Fletcher 2287
Fletcher Creek 4714
Flinders 2529
Flinders 3929
Flinders Park 5025
Flinders University 5042
Flinders View 4305
Flint 6302
Floraville 2280
Floreat 6014
Florey 2615
Flowerdale 3717
Flowerdale 7325
Flowerpot 7163
Flowery Gully 7270
Flying Fish Point 4860
Flynn 2615
Flynn 3844
Flynn 6302
Flynns Beach 2444
Footscray 3011

Forbes 2871
Forcett 7173
Fords Bridge 2840
Fordsdale 4343
Foreshores 4678
Forest 7330
Forest Grove 6286
Forest Hill 2651
Forest Hill 3131
Forest Hill 4342
Forest Hill 6324
Forest Lake 4078
Forest Range 5139
Forest Reefs 2798
Forest Ridge 4357
Forestdale 4118
Forestville 2087
Forestville 5035
Formartin 4404
Forrest 2603
Forrest 3236
Forrest 6434
Forrest Beach 6271
Forrestania 6359
Forrestdale 6112
Forresters Beach 2260
Forrestfield 6058
Forsayth 4871
Forster 2428
Fortescue 6716
Forth 7310
Fortitude Valley 4006
Foster 3960
Fosterville 3557
Foulden 4740
Fountain Gate 3805
Four Mile Creek 7215
Foxdale 4800
Foxground 2534

Framlingham 3265
Frances 5262
Frankford 7275
Frankland 6396
Franklin 7113
Franklinford 3461
Frankston 3199
Frankston North 3200
Fraser 2615
Fraser Range 6443
Frazerview 4309
Fredericksfield 4806
Frederickton 2440
Freeburgh 3741
Freeling 5372
Freemans Reach 2756
Freemans Waterhole
  2323
Freemantle 2795
Fregon 0872
Fremantle 6160
Fremantle private boxes
  6959
French Park 2655
Frenchman Bay 6330
Frenchs Forest private
  boxes 1640
Frenchs Forest 2086
Frenchville 4701
Freshwater 4870
Freshwater Creek 3216
Freshwater Point 4737
Frewville 5063
Friday Pocket 4855
Fryerstown 3451
Fulham 4313
Fulham 5024
Fulham Gardens 5024
Fullarton 5063

Fullerton 2583
Fullerton Cove 2318
Furnissdale 6210
Furracabad 2370
Fyansford 3221
Fyshwick 2609

G

Gabalong 6574
Gabbadah 6041
Gabbin 6476
Gaeta 4671
Gagebrook 7030
Gailes 4300
Gainsford 4702
Gairdner 6337
Gairloch 4850
Galiwinku 0822
Galong 2585
Galore 2652
Galston 2159
Ganmain 2702
Gap Ridge 6714
Gapsted 3737
Garah 2405
Garbutt 4814
Garden City 3207
Garden Island 6168
Garden Island Creek 7112
Garden Suburb 2289
Gardenvale 3185
Gardners Bay 7112
Garema 2871
Garfield 3814
Gargett 4741
Garland 2797
Garnant 4702
Garners Beach 4852
Garra 2866

Garradunga 4860
Garran 2605
Garthowen 2345
Garvoc 3265
Gascoyne Junction 6705
Gascoyne River 6705
Gateshead 2290
Gatton 4343
Gatton College 4345
Gatum 3407
Gaven 4211
Gawler 5118
Gawler 7315
Gawler Belt 5118
Gayndah 4625
Gaythorne 4051
Geebung 4034
Geelong 3220
Geelong West 3218
Geeveston 7116
Geham 4352
Geilston Bay 7015
Gelantipy 3885
Gellibrand 3239
Gellibrand Lower 3237
Gelliondale 3971
Gelorup 6230
Gemalla 2795
Gembrook 3783
Geneva 2474
Genoa 3891
Geographe 6280
George Town 7253
Georges Hall 2198
Georges Plains 2795
Georgetown 2298
Georgetown 4871
Georgetown 5472
Georgica 2480

Georgina 4825
Georgina 6532
Gepps Cross 5094
Geraldton 6530
Geralton private boxes 6531
Gerang Gerung 3418
Gerangamete 3243
Geranium 5301
Germantown 4871
Gerogeri 2642
Gerringong 2534
Gerroa 2534
Geurie 2831
Gheringhap 3331
Ghinghinda 4420
Ghinni Ghinni 2430
Ghooli 6426
Gibb 6743
Gibson 6448
Gidgegannup 6083
Gigoomgan 4620
Gilberton 4208
Gilberton 5081
Gilderoy 3797
Gilead 2560
Gilgai 2360
Gilgandra 2827
Gilgering 6302
Gilldora 4570
Gilles Plains 5086
Gillieston 3616
Gillieston Heights 2321
Gillimanning 6308
Gillingarra 6510
Gillman 5013
Gilmore 2720
Gilmore 2905
Gilston 4211

Gin Gin 4671
Gindoran 4676
Gingerah 6725
Gingin 6503
Ginginup 6503
Gingkin 2787
Ginninderra Village 2913
Ginoondan 4625
Gippsland mail centre 3841
Gipsy Point 3891
Giralang 2617
Girgarre 3624
Girilambone 2831
Girral 2669
Girraween 2145
Girrawheen 6064
Giru 4809
Girvan 2425
Gisborne 3437
Givelda 4670
Gladesville 1675
Gladesville 2111
Gladstone 2440
Gladstone 4680
Gladstone 5473
Gladstone 7264
Gladstone Park 3043
Gladysdale 3797
Glan Devon 4615
Glandore 5037
Glanmire 4570
Glanville 5015
Glass House Mountains 4518
Glaziers Bay 7109
Glebe 2037
Glebe 7000
Gledhow 6330

Glen Alpine 2560
Glen Alvie 3979
Glen Aplin 4381
Glen Boughton 4871
Glen Cairn 4342
Glen Creek 3691
Glen Davis 2846
Glen Echo 4570
Glen Eden 4680
Glen Esk 4312
Glen Forbes 3990
Glen Forrest 6071
Glen Huntly 3163
Glen Huon 7109
Glen Innes 2370
Glen Iris 3146
Glen Iris 6230
Glen Isla 4800
Glen Mervyn 6239
Glen Osmond 5064
Glen Ruth 4872
Glen Waverley 3150
Glen William 2321
Glenalta 5052
Glenarbon 4385
Glenaubyn 4424
Glenaven 4355
Glenbar 4620
Glenbrook 2773
Glenburn 3717
Glencoe 2365
Glencoe 5291
Glencoe 6316
Glendale 2285
Glendale 4711
Glendalough 6016
Glenden 4743
Glendenning 2761
Glendevie 7109

Glenelg 5045
Glenella 4740
Glenfern 7140
Glenfield 2167
Glenfield 6532
Glenfield Park 2650
Glenfyne 3266
Glengarry 3854
Glengarry 7275
Glengowrie 5044
Glenhaughton 4420
Glenhaven 2156
Glenlee 4711
Glenleigh 4630
Glenlusk 7012
Glenlynn 6256
Glenlyon 3461
Glenmaggie 3858
Glenmoral 4719
Glenmore 3340
Glenmore Park 2745
Glenmorgan 4423
Glennies Creek 2330
Glenning Valley 2261
Glenora 7140
Glenoran 6258
Glenorchy 3385
Glenorchy 4650
Glenorchy 7010
Glenore Grove 4342
Glenorie 2157
Glenrae 4626
Glenreagh 2450
Glenrock 4605
Glenrowan 3675
Glenroy 3046
Glenroy 4702
Glenside 5065
Glenthompson 3293

Glentromie 6509
Glenunga 5064
Glenvale 4350
Glenwood 2768
Glenwood 4570
Globe Derby Park 5110
Glossodia 2756
Glossop 5344
Gloucester 2422
Glynde 5070
Gnangara 6065
Gnarabup 6285
Gnarwarre 3221
Gnoorea 6714
Gnotuk 3260
Gnowangerup 6335
Gnowellen 6328
Gobur 3719
Godwin Beach 4511
Gogango 4702
Gol Gol 2738
Golconda 7254
Golden Bay 6174
Golden Beach 4551
Golden Fleece 4621
Golden Grove 5125
Golden Point 3350
Golden Point 3451
Golden Point 3465
Golden Square 3555
Golden Valley 7304
Goldsborough 3472
Goldsborough 4865
Golspie 2580
Good Night 4671
Goodar 4390
Goode Beach 6330
Goodger 4610
Goodlands 6468

Goodna 4300
Goodnight 2736
Goodooga 2831
Goodwood 4660
Goodwood 5034
Goodwood 7010
Googa Creek 4306
Goolboo 4856
Goolgowi 2652
Goolma 2852
Goolman 4306
Goolmangar 2480
Gooloogong 2805
Goolwa 5214
Goomalling 6460
Goomally 4702
Goomarin 6415
Goombungee 4354
Goomburra 4362
Goomeri 4601
Goomeribong 4601
Goondi 4860
Goondiwindi 4390
Goonellabah 2480
Goonengerry 2482
Goonumbla 2870
Gooram 3666
Gooramadda 3685
Goorambat 3725
Goorganga Creek 4800
Goorganga Plains 4800
Goornong 3557
Gooseberry Hill 6076
Gootchie 4650
Goovigen 4702
Goowarra 4702
Gorae 3305
Goranba 4421
Gordon 2072

Gordon 2906
Gordon 3345
Gordon 7150
Gordon Park 4031
Gordonbrook 4610
Gordonvale 4865
Gore 4352
Gorge Rock 6375
Gormandale 3873
Gorokan 2263
Goroke 3412
Gorrie 6556
Gosford 2250
Goshen 7216
Gosnells 6110
Gosnells 6990
Goughs Bay 3723
Goulburn 2580
Goulbourn Island 0822
Goulburn Weir 3608
Goulds Country 7216
Gowanbrae 3043
Gowangardie 3669
Gowrie 2340
Gowrie 2904
Gowrie Little Plain 4352
Gowrie Park 7306
Grabben Gullen 2583
Gracemere 4702
Gracetown 6284
Graceville 4075
Graceville East 4075
Grafton 2460
Grahams Creek 4650
Grahamstown 2729
Graman 2360
Granadilla 4855
Grand Secret 4820
Grandchester 4340

Grange 4051
Grange 5022
Grantham 4347
Granton 7030
Granville 2142
Grantville 3984
Granville 4650
Granville 6503
Granya 3701
Grapetree 4352
Grasmere 2570
Grass Patch 6446
Grass Valley 6403
Grassdale 4405
Grassmere 3275
Grasstree Beach 4740
Grasstree Hill 7017
Grassy 7256
Grassy Head 2441
Gravelly Beach 7276
Gravesend 2401
Gray 0830
Gray 7215
Grays Gate 4357
Grays Point 2232
Graytown 3608
Great Bay 7150
Great Keppel Island 4700
Great Sandy Straight
    4655
Great Western 3377
Gredgwin 3537
Green Fields 5107
Green Head 6514
Green Hills 2323
Green Hills 2730
Green Island 4871
Green Point 2251
Green Point 2428

Green Range 6328
Green Valley 2168
Green Valley 6330
Greenacre 2190
Greenacres 5086
Greenbank 4124
Greenbushes 6254
Greendale 2745
Greendale 3341
Greenethorpe 2809
Greenfield Park 2176
Greenfields 6210
Greenhill 2440
Greenhill 5140
Greenhills 6302
Greenlake 4701
Greenlands 2330
Greenmount 4359
Greenmount 4751
Greenmount 6056
Greenock 5360
Greenough 6530
Greens Beach 7270
Greens Creek 4570
Greensborough 3088
Greenslopes 4120
Greenup 4387
Greenvale 3059
Greenvale 4816
Greenway 2900
Greenways 5272
Greenwell Point 2540
Greenwich 2065
Greenwith 5125
Greenwood 4401
Greenwood 6024
Greenwood private
    boxes 6924
Geenwoods Valley 6405

Gregory 6535
Gregory River 4660
Gregory River 4800
Greigs Flat 2549
Grenfell 2810
Gresford 2311
Greta 2334
Greta 3675
Gretna 7140
Grevillia 2474
Grey 6521
Greycliffe 4715
Greys Plain 6701
Greystanes 2145
Griffin 4503
Griffith 2603
Griffith 2680
Grimwade 6253
Grindelwald 7277
Grogan 2666
Grong Grong 2652
Groomsville 4352
Grose Vale 2753
Grose Wald 2753
Grosmont 4419
Grosvenor 4627
Grosvenor Place 1220
Grove 7109
Grovedale 3216
Gruyere 3770
Guanaba 4210
Gubbata 2669
Guerilla Bay 2536
Guilderton 6041
Guildford 2161
Guildford 3451
Guildford 6055
Guildford private boxes
    6935

Gulargambone 2828
Gulfview Heights 5096
Gulgong 2852
Gulliver 4812
Gulnare 5471
Gulpa 2710
Guluguba 4418
Gum Flat 2360
Gum Scrub 2441
Gumdale 4154
Gumeracha 5233
Gumly Gumly 2652
Gunalda 4570
Gunbar 2711
Gunbower 3566
Gundagai 2722
Gundaring 6315
Gundaroo 2620
Gundiah 4650
Gundillion 2622
Gundowring 3691
Gundy 2337
Gungahlin 2912
Gungal 2333
Gungaloon 4620
Gunn 0832
Gunnawarra 4872
Gunnedah 2380
Gunnewin 4455
Gunning 2581
Gunningbland 2876
Gunns Plains 7315
Gununa 4871
Gunyarra 4800
Gunyidi 6513
Gurley 2398
Gurulmundi 4415
Gutha 6623
Guthalungra 4805

Guyra 2365
Guys Forest 3709
Guys Hill 3807
Gwabegar 2356
Gwambegwine 4420
Gwambygine 6302
Gwandalan 2259
Gwelup 6018
Gwindinup 6237
Gwynneville 2500
Gymbowen 3401
Gymea 2227
Gympie 4570

H

Haasts Bluff 0872
Habana 4740
Haberfield 2045
Hackett 2602
Hacketts Gully 6076
Hackham 5163
Hackney 5069
Haddon 3351
Haden 4352
Hadfield 3046
Hadspen 7290
Hagley 7292
Hahndorf 5245
Haigslea 4306
Hail Creek 4742
Halekulani 2262
Halfway Creek 2460
Haliday Bay 4740
Halifax 4850
Hall 2618
Hallam 3803
Hallett 5419
Hallett Cove 5158
Hallidays Point 2430

Halloran 2259
Halls Creek 6770
Halls Gap 3381
Halls Head 6210
Hallston 3953
Halton 2311
Haly Creek 4610
Hamel 6215
Hamelin Bay 6288
Hamelin Pool 6532
Hamersley 6022
Hamersley Range 6716
Hamilton 2303
Hamilton 3300
Hamilton 4007
Hamilton 5373
Hamilton 7140
Hamilton Creek 4714
Hamilton Hill 6163
Hamilton Hill private
  boxes 6963
Hamilton Island 4803
Hamilton Plains 4800
Hamley 5558
Hamley Bridge 5401
Hamlyn Heights 3215
Hamlyn Terrace 2259
Hammond 5431
Hammond Park 6164
Hammondville 2170
Hampden 4741
Hampshire 7321
Hampstead Gardens
  5086
Hampton 2790
Hampton 3188
Hampton Park 3976
Hannaford 4406
Hannam Vale 2443

Hannans 6430
Hannans private boxes
  6433
Hansonville 3675
Hanwood 2680
Happy Valley 4655
Happy Valley 4825
Happy Valley 5159
Harbord 2096
Harcourt 3453
Harden 2587
Hardys Bay 2257
Harefield 2650
Harford 7307
Hargraves 2850
Harkaway 3806
Harlaxton 4350
Harlin 4306
Harman 2600
Harper Creek 4552
Harrami 4630
Harriet 4625
Harrietville 3741
Harrington 2427
Harrington Park 2567
Harris Park 2150
Harris River 6225
Harrismith 6361
Harristown 4350
Harrisville 4307
Harrow 3317
Harston 3616
Hartley 2790
Harvey 6220
Harwood 2465
Haslam 5680
Hassall Grove 2761
Hastings 3915
Hastings 6308

Hastings 7109
Hastings Point 2489
Hat Head 2440
Hatfield 2715
Hatherleigh 5280
Havenview 7320
Havilah 2850
Hawker 2614
Hawker 5434
Hawkesbury Heights
  2777
Hawkesdale 3287
Hawkins Creek 4850
Hawks Nest 2324
Hawksburn 3142
Hawkwood 4626
Hawley Beach 7307
Hawthorn 3122
Hawthorn 5062
Hawthorn East 3123
Hawthorn South 3123
Hawthorndene 5051
Hawthorne 4171
Hay 2711
Hay 6333
Hay Point 4740
Hayborough 5211
Hayes 7140
Hayman Island 4801
Haymarket 1240
Haymarket 2000
Hazelbrook 2779
Hazeldean 4515
Hazeldene 3658
Hazelgrove 2787
Hazelmere 6055
Hazevale 6333
Hazelwood Park 5066
Hazledean 4741

Headington Hill 4361
Healesville 3777
Healy 4825
Heath Hill 3981
Heathcote 2233
Heathcote 3523
Heathcote Junction 3758
Heatherbrae 2324
Heatherton 3202
Heathfield 5153
Heathmont 3135
Heathpool 5068
Heathridge 6027
Heathwood 4110
Heatley 4814
Hebden 2330
Hebel 4486
Hebersham 2770
Heckenberg 2168
Hectorville 5073
Heddon Greta 2321
Hedley 3967
Heidelberg 3084
Heidelberg Heights 3081
Heidelberg West 3081
Helena Valley 6056
Helensburgh 2508
Helensvale 4210
Helidon 4344
Hemmant 4174
Henderson 6166
Hendon 5014
Hendra 4011
Henley 2111
Henley Beach 5022
Henley Brook 6055
Henty 2658
Henty 3312
Henty 6236

Hepburn Springs 3461
Herberton 4887
Herdsman 6017
Heritage Park 4118
Hermannsburg 0872
Hermidale 2831
Hermit Park 4812
Hernani 2453
Herne Hill 3218
Herne Hill 6056
Hernes Oak 3825
Heron Island 4680
Herons Creek 2443
Herrick 7264
Herron 6210
Herston 4006
Hervey Bay 4655
Hervey Range 4817
Hesket 3442
Hester 6255
Hewitt 2759
Hexham 2322
Hexham 3273
Heybridge 7316
Heyfield 3858
Heywood 3304
Hickety 6532
Hickeys Creek 2440
Hidden Valley 3756
Hidden Valley 4703
Hidden Valley 4816
Hideaway Bay 4800
Higgins 2615
Higginsville 6443
High Wycombe 6057
Highbury 5089
Highbury 6313
Highclere 7321
Highcroft 7183

Highett 3190
Highfields 4352
Highfields 2289
Highgate 5063
Highgate 6003
Highgate Hill 4101
Highgrove 4352
Highland Park 4211
Highland Plains 4401
Highland Plains 4454
Highpoint City 3032
Highton 3216
Highvale 4520
Hill End 2850
Hill End 3825
Hill River 6521
Hill Top 2575
Hillarys 6025
Hillarys 6923
Hillbank 5112
Hillcrest 3351
Hillcrest 4118
Hillcrest 5086
Hillcrest 7320
Hilldale 2420
Hillgrove 2350
Hillier 5116
Hillman 6168
Hillsborough 2290
Hillsborough 2320
Hillsdale 2036
Hillside 3037
Hillside 3875
Hillside 6312
Hillston 2675
Hilltown 5455
Hillwood 7252
Hilton 5033
Hilton 6163

Hilton Plaza 5033
Hinchinbrook 2168
Hindmarsh 5007
Hindmarsh 6462
Hines Hill 6413
Hinton 2321
Hithergreen 6280
Hivesville 4612
HMAS Albatross 2540
HMAS Cerberus 3920
HMAS Creswell 2540
Hobart 7000
Hobart private boxes
 7001
Hobartville 2753
Hobbys Yards 2795
Hocking 6065
Hoddles Creek 3139
Hoddys Well 6566
Hodleigh 4610
Hodgson 4455
Hoffman 6220
Holbrook 2644
Holden Hill 5088
Holder 2611
Holland Park 4121
Holleton 6426
Hollisdale 2446
Hollow Tree 7140
Holloways Beach 4878
Hollydeen 2333
Hollywell 4216
Holmesglen 3148
Holmesville 2286
Holmview 4207
Holmwood 6522
Holroyd 2142
Holsworthy 2173
Holt 2615

Holt Rock 6355
Holwell 7275
Holyoake 6213
Home Hill 4806
Home Island Cocos
 (Keeling) Islands 6799
Homebush 2140
Homebush 4740
Homebush Bay 2127
Homestead 4816
Homewood 3717
Honeywood 7017
Hookswood 4415
Hope Island 4212
Hope Valley 5090
Hope Valley 6165
Hopeland 4413
Hopeland 6125
Hopetoun 3396
Hopetoun 6348
Hopetoun Gardens 3162
Hoppers Crossing 3029
Hordern Vale 3238
Hornet Bank 4420
Horningsea Park 2171
Hornsby 1630
Hornsby 2077
Hornsby Westfield 1635
Horrocks 6535
Horse Camp 4671
Horse Creek 4714
Horseshoe Bay 4819
Horseshoe Lagoon 4809
Horsham 3400
Horsham private boxes
 3402
Horsley 2530
Horsley Park 2164
Horton 4660

Hotham Hill 3051
Hotham Heights 3741
Houghton 5131
Houston 3128
Hove 5048
Hovea 6071
Howard 4659
Howard Springs 0835
Howatharra 6532
Howden 7054
Howes Valley 2330
Howick 6450
Howlong 2643
Howrah 7018
Howth 7316
Hoxton Park 2171
Hoyleton 5453
Hudson 4860
Hughenden 4821
Hughes 2605
Hughesdale 3166
Hulongine 6460
Hume 2620
Hume Weir 3691
Humeburn 4490
Humevale 3757
Humphrey 4625
Humpy Doo 0836
Humula 2652
Hunchy 4555
Hungerford 4493
Hunter 3558
Hunter Region 2310
Hunters Hill 2110
Huntfield Heights 5163
Huntingdale 3166
Huntingdale 6110
Huntingdon 2446
Huntingfield 7055

Huntleys Cove 2111
Huntleys Point 2111
Huntly 3551
Huon 3695
Huonville 7109
Hurlstone Park 2193
Hurstbridge 3099
Hurstville 2220
Hurstville 1481
Huskisson 2540
Hutton Creek 4454
Hyams Beach 2540
Hyde Park 4812
Hyde Park 5061
Hyden 6359
Hynam 5262

I
Idalia 4811
Ideraway 4625
Ikewa 6522
Ilford 2850
Ilfracombe 4727
Ilkley 4554
Illabarook 3351
Illabo 2590
Illawong 2234
Illowa 3282
Iluka 2466
Iluka 6028
Imbil 4570
Inala 4077
Indee 6721
Indented Head 3223
Indooroopilly 4068
Inggarda 6701
Ingham 4850
Ingle Farm 5098
Ingleburn 1890

Ingleburn 2565
Inglehope 6213
Ingleside 2101
Inglewood 3517
Inglewood 4387
Inglewood 5133
Inglewood 6052
Inglewood private boxes
    6932
Ingoldsby 4343
Injune 4454
Inkerman 3472
Inkerman 4806
Inkpen 6302
Inman Valley 5211
Innaloo 6018
Innaloo private boxes
    6918
Innawanga 6751
Innisfail 4860
Innot Hot Springs 4872
Inskip 4581
Interlaken 7120
Inverell 2360
Invergordon 3636
Invergordon South 3634
Invergowrie 2350
Inverlaw 4610
Inverleigh 3321
Inverloch 3996
Invermay 3352
Invermay 7248
Inverness 4703
Iona 3815
Ipswich 4305
Iredale 4352
Irishtown 6401
Irishtown 7330
Iron Baron 5600

Iron Knob 5601
Ironbank 5153
Ironbark 4306
Irongate 4356
Ironpot 4610
Irrewarra 3249
Irvinebank 4872
Irvingdale 4404
Irvington 2470
Irwin 6525
Irymple 3498
Isaacs 2607
Isabela 2795
Isabella Plains 2905
Isis Central 4660
Isisford 4721
Isla 4719
Isle Of Capri 4217
Islington 2296
Israelite Bay 6452
Issenka 6535
Ivanhoe 2878
Ivanhoe 3079
Iveragh 4680

J
Jabiru 0886
Jabuk 5301
Jacana 3047
Jackadgery 2460
Jackeys Marsh 7304
Jackitup 6335
Jackson 4426
Jacobs Well 4208
Jacup 6337
Jaffa 4855
Jalbarragup 6275
Jaloran 6315
Jam Jerrup 3984

Jamberoo 2533
Jambin 4702
Jamboree Heights 4074
James Cook University
    4811
Jamestown 5491
Jamieson 3723
Jamison Centre 2614
Jan Juc 3228
Jancourt East 3266
Jandabup 6065
Jandakot 6164
Jandowae 4410
Jane Brook 6056
Jannali 2226
Jardee 6258
Jardine 4702
Jarklin 3517
Jarrahdale 6124
Jarrahwood 6275
Jarvisfield 4807
Jaspers Brush 2535
Jeeralang 3840
Jeetho 3945
Jelcobine 6306
Jellinbah 4702
Jembaicumbene 2622
Jennacubbine 6401
Jennapullin 6401
Jenolan Caves 2790
Jeogla 2350
Jeparit 3423
Jerangle 2630
Jerdacuttup
Jeremadra 2536
Jericho 4728
Jericho 5554
Jericho 7030
Jerilderie 2716

Keith 5267
Keith Hall 2478
Kellerberrin 6410
Kellevie 7176
Kellyville 2155
Kelmscott 6111
Kelmscott private boxes 1-550 6991
Kelmscott private boxes 1001-1240 6997
Kelsey Creek 4800
Kelso 2795
Kelso 4815
Kelso 7270
Kelvin 2380
Kelvin Grove 4059
Kelvinhaugh 4401
Kembla Grange 2526
Kemblawarra 2505
Kemmis 4742
Kemps Creek 2171
Kempsey 2440
Kempton 7030
Kendall 2439
Kendenup 6323
Kenebri 2396
Kenilworth 4574
Kenmare 6316
Kenmore 4069
Kennedy 4816
Kennedy Range 6701
Kennedys Creek 3239
Kennett River 3221
Kennington 3550
Kensington 1465
Kensington 2033
Kensington 3031
Kensington 4670
Kensington 5068

Kensington 6151
Kensington Grove 4341
Kent Town 5067
Kent Town private boxes 5071
Kentdale 6333
Kenthurst 2156
Kentlyn 2560
Kentucky 2354
Kenwick 6107
Keon Park 3073
Keperra 4054
Kepnock 4670
Keppel Sands 4702
Kerang 3579
Kergunyah 3691
Kernot 3979
Kerrabee 2328
Kerrie 3434
Kerrimuir 3129
Kerrisdale 3660
Kerrsbrook 5231
Keswick 5035
Kettering 7155
Kew 2439
Kew 3101
Kew East 3102
Kewarra Beach 4879
Kewdale 6105
Keyneton 5353
Keysborough 3173
Keysbrook 6126
Keysland 4612
Khancoban 2642
Kholo 4306
Ki Ki 5261
Kia Ora 4570
Kiah 2551
Kialla 2583

Kialla 3631
Kiama 2533
Kianga 4718
Kiara 6054
Kiata 3418
Kidman Park 5025
Kielpa 5642
Kiels Mountain 4559
Kiewa 3691
Kilaben Bay 2283
Kilburn 5084
Kilcoy 4515
Kilcunda 3995
Kilkenny 5009
Kilkivan 4600
Killabakh 2429
Killara 2071
Killara 3312
Killara 3691
Killarney 3282
Killarney 4373
Killarney Heights 2087
Killarney Vale 2261
Killcare 2257
Killiecrankie 7255
Killingworth 2278
Killora 7150
Kilmany 3851
Kilmore 3764
Kilsyth 3137
Kimba 5641
Kimberley 7304
Kimbriki 2429
Kin Kin 4571
Kin Kora 4680
Kinbombi 4601
Kinchant Dam 4741
Kincora 4356
Kincumber 2251

Kindon 4390
Kindred 7310
King River 6330
King Scrub 4521
Kingaroy 4610
Kinglake 3763
Kinglake West 3757
Kingoonya 5710
Kings Beach 4551
Kings Creek 2446
Kings Creek 4361
Kings Cross 1340
Kings Langley 2147
Kings Meadows 7249
Kings Park 2148
Kings Park 5034
Kings Park 3021
Kings Park 6005
Kingsbury 3083
Kingscliff 2487
Kingscote 5223
Kingsdale 2580
Kingsdene 2118
Kingsford 2032
Kingsford 5118
Kingsford 6701
Kingsgrove 1480
Kingsgrove 2208
Kingsholme 4208
Kingsley 6026
Kingsthorpe 4400
Kingston 2604
Kingston 3364
Kingston 4114
Kingston 6256
Kingston 7050
Kingston private boxes 7051
Kingston Beach 7050

Kingston-On-Murray 5331
Kingston Park 5049
Kingston S.E. 5275
Kingstown 2358
Kingsvale 2587
Kingsville 3012
Kingsway 6065
Kingsway West 2208
Kingswood 2340
Kingswood 2550
Kingswood 2747
Kingswood 5062
Kinkuna 4670
Kinross 6028
Kintore 0872
Kioloa 2539
Kioma 4498
Kiora 2537
Kippa-ring 4021
Kippax 2615
Kirk Rock 6370
Kirknie 4806
Kirkstall 3282
Kirkwood 4680
Kirrama 4872
Kirrawee 2232
Kirribilli 2061
Kirup 6251
Kirwan 4817
Kitchener 2325
Kithbrook 3666
Kitoba 4605
Kleinton 4352
Klemzig 5087
Knorrit Flat 2424
Knowsley 3523
Knox City Centre 3152
Knoxfield 3180

Kobble Creek 4520
Koetong 3704
Kogan 4406
Kogarah 1485
Kogarah 2217
Kojaneerup South 6328
Kojarena 6532
Kojonup 6395
Kokeby 6304
Kokotungo 4702
Kolodong 2430
Kolonga 4671
Kolora 3265
Kondinin 6367
Kondut 6605
Kongorong 5291
Kongwak 3951
Konnongorring 6603
Koo Wee Rup 3981
Koojan 6510
Kookynie 6431
Koolan Island 6733
Koolanooka 6623
Koolewong 2256
Koolunga 5464
Koolyanobbing 6427
Koomberkine 6461
Koombooloomba 4872
Koonawarra 2530
Koonda 3669
Koondoola 6064
Koondrook 3580
Koongal 4701
Koongamia 6056
Koonwarra 3954
Koonya 7187
Kooragang 2304
Koorainghat 2430
Kooralbyn 4285

Kooralgin 4402
Koorawatha 2807
Koorda 6475
Kooringal 2650
Kooringal 4025
Koorlong 3501
Koornalla 3844
Kooroona 5558
Kooroongarra 4357
Kootingal 2352
Kooyong 3144
Koraleigh 2735
Korbel 6415
Kordabup 6333
Koriella 3714
Korobeit 3341
Koroit 3282
Korong Vale 3520
Korora 2450
Korrelocking 6485
Korumburra 3950
Korweinguboora 3461
Kotara 2289
Kotara East 2305
Kotara Fair 2289
Kotta 3565
Kotupna 3638
Koumala 4738
Kowanyama 4871
Kowguran 4415
Koyuga 3622
Koyuga South 3621
Krambach 2429
Krondorf 5352
Kronkup 6330
Krowera 3945
Kudardup 6290
Kudla 5115
Kuender 6353

Kukerin 6352
Kulikup 6244
Kulin 6365
Kulja 6470
Kullogum 4660
Kulnura 2250
Kulpi 4352
Kumbarina 6642
Kumbia 4610
Kunda Park 4556
Kundabung 2441
Kunghur 2484
Kunioon 4615
Kunjin 6375
Kununoppin 6489
Kununurra 6743
Kunyung 3930
Kuraby 4112
Kuranda 4872
Kurmond 2757
Kurnalpi 6431
Kurnell 2231
Kurrajong 2758
Kurralta Park 5037
Kurrenkutten 6375
Kurri Kurri 2327
Kurrimine Beach 4871
Kurrowah 4352
Kurumbul 4388
Kurunjang 3337
Kurwongbah 4503
Kuttabul 4741
Kweda 6306
Kwelkan 6490
Kwinana 6966
Kwinana Beach 6167
Kwinana Town Centre
   6167
Kwolyin 6385

Kyabram 3620
Kyabram private boxes
   3619
Kyalite 2734
Kyancutta 5651
Kybybolite 5262
Kyeemagh 2216
Kyle Bay 2221
Kyneton 3444
Kynuna 4823
Kyogle 2474
Kyoomba 4380

L
La Perouse 2036
La Trobe University 3083
Laanecoorie 3463
Labertouche 3816
Labrador 4215
Laburnum 3130
Laceys Creek 4521
Lachlan 7140
Lackrana 7255
Lady Barron 7255
Ladysmith 2652
Laggan 2583
Lagrange 6725
Laguna 2325
Laguna Quays 4800
Laidley 4341
Lajamanu 0852
Lake Albert 2650
Lake Argyle 6743
Lake Austin 6640
Lake Bathurst 2580
Lake Biddy 6355
Lake Boga 3584
Lake Bolac 3351
Lake Borumba 4570

Lake Brown 6479
Lake Camm 6355
Lake Cargelligo 2672
Lake Carnegie 6646
Lake Cathie 2445
Lake Charm 3581
Lake Clarendon 4343
Lake Clifton 6215
Lake Conjola 2539
Lake Darlot 6438
Lake Deborah 6484
Lake Grace 6353
Lake Haven 2263
Lake Heights 2502
Lake Hinds 6603
Lake Illawarra 2528
Lake Jasper 6260
Lake King 6356
Lake Leake 7210
Lake Macdonald 4563
Lake Manchester 4306
Lake Margarette 6475
Lake Mary 4703
Lake Monduran 4671
Lake Muir 6258
Lake Mundi 3312
Lake Munmorah 2259
Lake Ninan 6603
Lake Proserpine 4800
Lake Rowan 3727
Lake St Clair 7140
Lake Tabourie 2539
Lake Tinaroo 4872
Lake Toolbrunup 6320
Lake Tyers 3887
Lake Tyers Beach 3909
Lake View 5555
Lake Wells 6440
Lake Wendouree 3350

Lake Wyangan 2680
Lakelands 2282
Lakelands 6210
Lakemba 2195
Lakes Entrance 3909
Lakesland 2572
Lakewood 6431
Lal Lal 3352
Lalbert 3542
Lalla 7267
Lalor 3075
Lalor Park 2147
Lamb Island 4184
Lambton 2299
Lameroo 5302
Lamington 6430
Lamington National
  Park 4275
Lammermoor 4703
Lancaster 3620
Lancefield 3435
Lancelin 6044
Landsborough 3384
Landsborough 4550
Landsdale 6065
Lane 1595
Lane Cove 2066
Lanefield 4340
Lanena 7275
Lang Lang 3984
Lange 6330
Langford 6147
Langhorne Creek 5255
Langkoop 3312
Langley 4630
Langley Vale 2426
Langwarrin 3910
Langwarrin 3911
Lansdowne 2430

Lansvale 2166
Lapoinya 7325
Lapstone 2773
Lara 3212
Larapinta 4110
Largs 2320
Largs Bay 5016
Largs North 5016
Larpent 3249
Larrakeyah 0820
Larras Lee 2866
Larrimah 0852
Lascelles 3487
Latham 2615
Latham 6616
Lathlain 6100
Latrobe 7307
Lauderdale 7021
Laughtondale 2775
Launceston 7250
Launching Place 3139
Laura 4871
Laura 5480
Laurel Hill 2649
Laurieton 2443
Lavelle 4357
Lavender Bay 2060
Lavers Hill 3238
Laverton 3028
Laverton 6440
Laverton North 3026
Lavington 2641
Lavington private boxes
  2640
Law Courts Vic. private
  boxes 8010
Lawes 4343
Lawgi Dawes 4716
Lawloit 2418

Lawnton 4501
Lawrence 2460
Lawson 2617
Lawson 2783
Leabrook 5068
Leadville 2831
Leafdale 4606
Leanyer 0812
Learmonth 3352
Learmonth 6707
Leawood Gardens 5150
Lebrina 7254
Leda 6170
Ledge Point 6043
Lee Point 0810
Leederville 6007
Leederville private boxes
  1-125 6902
Leederville private boxes
  126-575 6903
Leeman 6514
Leeming 6149
Leeton 2705
Leeuwin 6290
Leeville 2470
Lefroy 7252
Lefthand Branch 4343
Legana 7277
Legerwood 7263
Legume 2476
Leichardt 3516
Leichhardt 2040
Leichhardt 4305
Leigh Creek 3352
Leigh Creek 5731
Leinster 6437
Leitchville 3567
Leith 7315
Lemnos 3631

Lemon Tree 2259
Lemon Tree Passage
  2319
Lemont 7120
Lemontree 4357
Lenaghan 2322
Lenah Valley 7008
Leneva 3691
Lennard Brook 6503
Lennox Head 2478
Lenswood 5240
Leonay 2750
Leongatha 3953
Leonora 6438
Leopold 3224
Leppington 2179
Lerderderg 3458
Leschenault 6233
Lesley 6111
Leslie Vale 7054
Lesmurdie 6076
Lethbridge 3332
Lethbridge Park 2770
Lethebrook 4800
Leumeah 2560
Leura 2780
Levendale 7120
Lewisham 2049
Lewisham 7173
Lewiston 5501
Lexia 6065
Lexton 3352
Leyburn 4352
Leydens Hill 4714
Licola 3858
Lidcombe 1825
Lidcombe 2141
Liddell 2333
Lidsdale 2790

Lietinna 7261
Liffey 7301
Lightning Ridge 2834
Lileah 7330
Lilli Pilli 2229
Lilli Pilli 2536
Lillico 7310
Lillimur 3415
Lilliput 3682
Lilydale 3140
Lilydale 4344
Lilydale 7268
Lilyfield 2040
Lilyvale 4352
Lima 3673
Limbri 2352
Lime Lake 6315
Limeburners Creek 2324
Limerick 2583
Limestone 4714
Limestone Creek 4701
Limestone Ridges 4305
Limevale 4384
Lindeman Island 4741
Linden 2778
Linden 4490
Linden Park 5065
Lindenow 3865
Lindenow South 3875
Lindfield 2070
Lindisfarne 7015
Linfarne 6258
Linley Point 2066
Linthorpe 4356
Linton 3360
Linville 4306
Linwood 5410
Lisarow 2250
Lisle 7254

Lismore 2480
Lismore 3324
Lissner 4820
Liston 2372
Litchfield 3480
Lithgow 2790
Littabella 4673
Little Bay 2036
Little Grove 6330
Little Hartley 2790
Little Italy 6355
Little Mountain 4551
Little Plain 2360
Little River 3211
Little Sandy Desert 6646
Little Swanport 7190
Littlehampton 5250
Liverpool 1871
Liverpool 2170
Llandilo 2747
Llanelly 3551
Llangothlin 2365
Lobethal 5241
Loccota 7255
Loch 3945
Loch Sport 3851
Lochiel 5510
Lochinvar 2321
Lock 5633
Lockhart 2656
Lockhart 4871
Lockier 6522
Lockington 3563
Lockleys 5032
Lockridge 6054
Locksley 2795
Locksley 3665
Lockwood South 3551
Lockyer 4344

Lockyer 6330
Lockyer Waters 4311
Loftus 2232
Logan 3475
Logan Central 4114
Logan Reserve 4133
Logan Village 4207
Loganholme 4129
Loganlea 4131
Loira 7275
Lol Gray 6311
Londonderry 2753
Londonderry 6429
Lone Pine 3691
Lonesome Creek 4719
Long Beach 2536
Long Flat 2446
Long Flat 4570
Long Gully 3550
Long Island 4741
Long Jetty 2261
Long Point 2564
Longford 3851
Longford 7301
Longlea 3551
Longley 7150
Longreach 4730
Longueville 2066
Longwarry 3816
Longwood 3665
Longwood 5153
Lonnavale 7109
Lonsdale 5160
Lord Howe Island 2898
Lorinna 7306
Lorn 2320
Lorne 2439
Lorne 3232
Lort River 6447

Lostock 2311
Lota 4179
Lottah 7216
Lotus Creek 4705
Louth 2840
Louth Bay 5607
Loveday 5345
Lovely Banks 3221
Lovett Bay 2105
Low Head 7253
Lowanna 2450
Lowbank 5320
Lowden 6240
Lower Chittering 6084
Lower Cowley 4871
Lower Creek 2440
Lower Cressbrook 4313
Lower Hawkesbury 2775
Lower Hermitage 5131
Lower Hotham 6390
Lower King 6330
Lower Light 5501
Lower Longley 7109
Lower Mangrove 2250
Lower Marshes 7030
Lower Mitcham 5062
Lower Mount Walker
  4340
Lower Plenty 3093
Lower Portland 2756
Lower Tenthill 4343
Lowesdale 2646
Lowlands 6330
Lowmead 4676
Lowood 4311
Lowther 2790
Loxford 2326
Loxton 5333
Loyetea 7316

Lubeck 3381
Lucas Heights 2234
Lucaston 7109
Lucinda 4850
Lucindale 5272
Lucknow 2800
Lucknow 3875
Lucyvale 3691
Luddenham 2745
Ludlow 6271
Ludmilla 0820
Lue 2850
Lugarno 2210
Lughrata 7255
Lulworth 7252
Lumeah 4478
Lumeah 6395
Lunawanna 7150
Lundavra 4390
Lune River 7109
Lurnea 2170
Luscombe 4207
Lutana 7009
Lutwyche 4030
Lyalls Mill 6225
Lymington 7109
Lynbrook 3975
Lynchs Creek 2474
Lyndhurst 2797
Lyndhurst 3975
Lyndhurst 5731
Lyndoch 5351
Lyndon 6701
Lyneham 2602
Lynford 4342
Lynton 5062
Lynwood 6147
Lyons 2606
Lyonville 3461

Lyra 4352
Lyrup 5343
Lysterfield 3156
Lytton 4178

M

Ma Ma Creek 4347
Maadi 4855
Mabins Well 2716
Macalister 4406
Macarthur 2904
Macarthur 3286
Macclesfield 3782
Macclesfield 5153
MacDonald Park 5121
Macedon 3440
Macfarlane 4478
MacGregor 2615
MacGregor 4109
MacHans Beach 4878
Machine Creek 4695
Mackay 4740
Mackenzie 4156
Mackenzie 4702
Mackenzie River 4705
MacKnade 4850
Macks Creek 3971
Macksville 2447
Maclagan 4352
Maclean 2463
MacLeay Island 4184
Macleod 3085
Macleod 6701
MacMasters Beach 2251
Macorna 3578
Macquarie 2614
Macquarie 7151
Macquarie Centre 2113
Macquarie Fields 2564

Macquarie Island 7150
Macquarie Links 2565
Macquarie Park 2113
Macquarie Plains 7140
Macquarie University 2109
Macrossan 4816
Maddington 6109
Maddington private boxes 6989
Madeley 6065
Madora Bay 6210
Madura 6443
Maffra 3860
Magenta 6355
Magill 5072
Magitup 6338
Magnetic Island 4819
Magpie 3352
Magra 7140
Mahogany Creek 6072
Mahomets Flats 6530
Maianbar 2230
Maida Vale 6057
Maiden Gully 3551
Maidenhead 4385
Maidenwell 4615
Maidstone 3012
Main Beach 4217
Main Ridge 3928
Maitland 2320
Maitland 5573
Maitland 6714
Majorca 3465
Majors Creek 2622
Malabaine 6401
Malabar 2036
Malaga 6090

Malaga private boxes 6944
Malak 0812
Malanda 4885
Malarga 4620
Malbina 7140
Maldon 3463
Malebelling 6302
Maleny 4552
Mallabula 2319
Mallacoota 3892
Mallala 5502
Mallanganee 2469
Mallee Hill 6353
Malling 4352
Malmalling 6556
Malmoe 4627
Malmsbury 3446
Maloneys Beach 2536
Malu 4403
Malua Bay 2536
Malvern 3144
Malvern 5061
Malvern East 3145
Malyalling 6370
Mambray Creek 5495
Manahan 2200
Manangatang 3546
Manapouri 4361
Mandagery 2870
Madalay 4802
Mandalong 2264
Mandogalup 6167
Mandurah 6210
Mandurama 2792
Mandurang 3551
Maneroo 4730
Mangalore 3663
Mangalore 7030

Mangana 7214
Mangerton 2500
Mango Hill 4503
Mangoplah 2652
Mangrove Mountain 2250
Manifold Heights 3218
Manildra 2865
Manilla 2346
Maningrida 0822
Manjimup 6258
Manly 1655
Manly 2095
Manly 4179
Manly Vale 2093
Manly West 4179
Manmanning 6465
Manna Hill 5440
Mannerim 3222
Mannering Park 2259
Manning 6152
Manning Point 2430
Manningham 5086
Mannuem 4610
Mannum 5238
Manoora 4870
Manoora 5414
Mansfield 3722
Mansfield private boxes 3724
Mansfield 4122
Mansfield Park 5012
Manuka 2603
Manunbar 4601
Manunda 4870
Manyana 2539
Manypeaks 6328
Manyung 4601

Mapleton 4560
Marama 5307
Marananga 5355
Maranboy 0852
Marangaroo 6064
Maranup 6256
Maraylya 2765
Marayong 2148
Marbelup 6330
Marble Bar 6760
Marburg 4346
March 2800
Marchagee 6515
Marcoola 4564
Marcus Beach 4573
Marcus Hill 3222
Mardella 6125
Marden 5070
Mardi 2259
Mardie 6714
Mareeba 4880
Margaret River 6285
Margate 4019
Margate 7054
Margate Beach 4019
Maria Creeks 4855
Marian 4753
Maribyrnong 3032
Mariginiup 6065
Marino 5049
Marion 5043
Marion Bay 5575
Marion Bay 7175
Marks Point 2280
Markwell 2423
Marla 5724
Marlborough 4705
Marlee 2429
Marleston 5033

Marlo 3888
Marlow Lagoon 0830
Marmion 6020
Marmong Point 2284
Marne 6608
Marnoo 3387
Marodian 4570
Marom Creek 2480
Marong 3515
Maroochy River 4561
Maroochydore 4558
Maroona 3377
Maroondan 4671
Maroota 2756
Maroubra 2035
Marrabel 5413
Marracoonda 6317
Marradong 6390
Marrah 6532
Marrangaroo 2790
Marrar 2652
Marrara 0812
Marrawah 7330
Marree 5733
Marrickville 1475
Marrickville 2204
Marrinup 6213
Marryatville 5068
Marsden 4132
Marsden Park 2765
Marsfield 2122
Marshall 3216
Marshdale 2420
Marshlands 4611
Martin 6110
Martinsville 2265
Martynvale 4870
Martyville 4858
Marulan 2579

Marungi 3634
Marvel Loch 6426
Maryborough 3465
Maryborough 4650
Marybrook 6280
Maryknoll 3812
Maryland 2287
Marys Creek 4570
Marysville 3779
Maryvale 2820
Maryvale 4370
Maryvale 4703
Maryville 2293
Mascot 1460
Mascot 2020
Maslin Beach 5170
Massey Bay 6701
Mataranka 0852
Matcham 2250
Matheson 2370
Mathinna 7214
Mathoura 2710
Matlock 3723
Matong 2652
Matraville 2036
Matta Flat 5554
Maude 2711
Maude 3331
Maudsland 4210
Mawbanna 7321
Mawson 2607
Mawson 7150
Mawson Lakes 5095
May Downs 4746
Maya 6614
Mayanup 6244
Mayberry 7304
Maydena 7140
Mayfield 2304

Mayfield 2622
Mayfield 7248
Maylands 5069
Maylands 6051
Maylands private boxes
    6931
Mayrung 2710
Mays Hill 2145
McAlinden 6225
McBeath 6770
McCracken 5211
McCrae 3938
McCullys Gap 2333
McCutcheon 4856
McDesme 4807
McDowell 4053
McEwens Beach 4740
McGraths Hill 2756
McIlwraith 4671
McIntosh Creek 4671
McKail 6330
McKees Hill 2480
McKellar 2617
McKinlay 4823
McKinnon 3204
McLaren Flat 5171
McLaren Vale 5171
McMahons Creek 3799
McMahons Point 2060
Meadow Flat 2795
Meadow Heights 3048
Meadow Springs 6210
Meadowbank 2114
Meadowbrook 4131
Meadows 5201
Meadowvale 4670
Meandarra 4422
Meander 7304
Meckering 6405

Medina 6167
Medindie 5081
Medlow Bath 2780
Medowie 2318
Meekatharra 6642
Meelon 6208
Meenaar 6401
Meeniyan 3956
Meering West 3579
Meerlieu 3862
Meerschaum Vale 2477
Megalong 2785
Megan 2453
Meikleville Hill 4703
Melaleuca 6065
Melawondi 4570
Melba 2615
Melbourne City 3000
Melbourne 3004
Melbourne private boxes
    3001
Melbourne Airport 3045
Melbourne University
    3052
Mella 7330
Melrose 4613
Melrose 5483
Melrose 7310
Melrose Park 2114
Melrose Park 5039
Melton 3337
Melton Mowbray 7030
Melton South 3338
Melville 2759
Melville 6156
Melville Forest 3315
Memana 7255
Mena Creek 4871
Menai 2234

Menangle 2568
Menangle Park 2563
Mendooran 2842
Mengha 7330
Menindee 2879
Meningie 5264
Menora 6050
Mentmore 4798
Mentone 3194
Menzies 4825
Menzies 6436
Menzies Creek 3159
Mepunga 3277
Merbein 3505
Meredith 3333
Merewether 2291
Merilup 6352
Merimbula 2548
Merinda 4805
Meringandan 4352
Meringo 2537
Meringur 3496
Merino 3310
Merivale 6450
Merkanooka 6625
Merlwood 4605
Merlynston 3058
Mermaid Beach 4218
Mernda 3754
Meroo Meadow 2540
Merredin 6415
Merricks 3916
Merricks Beach 3926
Merricks North 3926
Merrigum 3618
Merrijig 3723
Merrimac 4226
Merriton 5523
Merritts Creek 4352

Merriwa 2329
Merriwa 6030
Merriwagga 2652
Merrygoen 2831
Merrylands 2160
Merryvale 4340
Mersey Forest 7304
Merseylea 7305
Merton 3715
Meru 6530
Metcalfe 3448
Metford 2323
Metricup 6280
Mettler 6328
Metung 3904
Meunna 7325
Mia Mia 3444
Mia Mia 4754
Miami 4220
Miamoon 6612
Miandetta 2825
Miandetta 7310
Miara 4673
Mica Creek 4825
Michelago 2620
Mickleham 3064
Mid Valley 3840
Middle Beach 5501
Middle Camberwell 3124
Middle Camp 2281
Middle Cove 2068
Middle Park 3206
Middle Park 4074
Middle Ridge 4350
Middle Swan 6056
Middlemount 4746
Middlesex 6258
Middleton 4735
Middleton 5213

Middleton 7163
Middleton Beach 6330
Middleton Grange 2171
Midgee 4702
Midgeree Bar 4852
Midland 6056
Midvale 6056
Midway Point 7171
Miena 7030
Mighell 4860
Mila 2632
Milabena 7325
Milang 5256
Milawa 3678
Milbrulong 2656
Mildura 3500
Mildura private boxes
 3502
Mile End 5031
Miles 4415
Miles End 4825
Miling 6575
Milingimbi 0822
Mill Park 3082
Millaa Millaa 4886
Millaroo 4807
Millars Well 6714
Millbank 2440
Millbank 4670
Millbridge 6232
Millbrook 3352
Millbrook 6330
Millchester 4820
Mil-lel 5291
Millendon 6056
Miller 2168
Millers Forest 2324
Millers Point 2000
Millfield 2325

Millgrove 3799
Millicent 5280
Millmerran 4357
Millner 0810
Milloo 3572
Mills Lake
Millstream 4888
Millstream 6716
Millswood 5034
Millthorpe 2798
Millwood 4357
Milo 6525
Milpara 2880
Milperra 1891
Milperra 2214
Milsons Passage 2083
Milsons Point 1565
Milsons Point 2061
Milton 2538
Milton 4064
Milvale 2594
Mimegarra 6507
Mimosa 4702
Min min 4829
Mincha 3575
Minchinbury 2770
Mindarabin 6336
Mindarie 6030
Mindarra 6503
Minden 4340
Minding 6315
Miners Rest 3352
Mingela 4816
Mingenew 6522
Mingo 4625
Minhamite 3287
Minigin 6312
Minilya 6701
Minimay 3413

Mininera 3351
Minjilang 0822
Minlaton 5575
Minmi 2287
Minnamoolka 4872
Minnamurra 2533
Minnenooka 6532
Minnie Downs 4478
Minnipa 5654
Minnivale 6462
Mintabie 5724
Mintaro 5415
Minto 2566
Minyama 4575
Minyip 3392
Minyirr 6725
Mira Mar 6330
Miram 3415
Miranda 1490
Miranda 2228
Mirani 4754
Mirannie 2330
Mirboo North 3871
Miriam Vale 4677
Mirimbah 3722
Miriwinni 4871
Mirrabooka 2264
Mirrabooka 6061
Mirrabooka private
 boxes 6941
Mirrool 2665
Missabotti 2449
Missen Flat 4361
Missenden Road 2050
Mission Beach 4852
Mitcham 3132
Mitcham 5062
Mitchell 0832
Mitchell 2911

Mitchell 4465
Mitchell Park 3352
Mitchell Park 3355
Mitchell Park 5043
Mitchell Plateau 6740
Mitchells Flat 2330
Mitchelton 4053
Mitiamo 3573
Mitre 3401
Mitta Mitta 3701
Mittagong 2575
Miva 4570
Moama 2731
Moana 5169
Mobrup 6395
Mocardy 6603
Moculta 5353
Modbury 5092
Modella 3816
Modewarre 3240
Moe 3825
Moffat Beach 4551
Moffatdale 4605
Mogareeka 2550
Mogendoura 2537
Moggill 4070
Moggs Creek 3231
Mogo 2536
Mogriguy 2830
Mogumber 6506
Moil 0810
Moina 7310
Moira 2710
Mokine 6401
Molangul 4671
Mole Creek 7304
Molendinar 4214
Molesworth 3718
Molesworth 7140

Moliagul 3472
Mollerin 6471
Mollongghip 3352
Molloy Island 6290
Mollymook 2539
Molong 2866
Moltema 7304
Molyullah 3673
Mona Park4807
Mona Vale 1660
Mona Vale 2103
Monak 2738
Monal 4630
Monarto South 5254
Monash 2904
Monash 5342
Monash Park 2111
Monash University 3800
Monbulk 3793
Monduran 4671
Mondure 4611
Monga 2622
Mongarlowe 2622
Mongogarie 2470
Monjebup 6338
Monjingup 6450
Monkerai 2415
Monkey Mia 6537
Monkland 4570
Monogorilby 4626
Monomeith 3984
Monsildale 4515
Mont Albert 3127
Mont Albert North 3129
Montacute 5134
Montagu 7330
Montagu Bay 7018
Montana 7304
Monteagle 2594

Montello 7320
Monterey 2217
Montmorency 3094
Monto 4630
Montrose 3765
Montrose 7010
Montville 4560
Mooball 2483
Moodiarrup 6393
Mooga 4455
Moogara 7140
Moojebing 6317
Moolap 3221
Moolboolaman 4671
Mooliabeenee 6504
Mooloo 4570
Mooloolaba 4557
Mooloolah 4553
Moombooldool 2665
Moombra 4312
Moomin 4887
Moonah 7009
Moonambel 3478
Moonan Brook 2337
Moonan Flat 2337
Moonbi 2353
Moondah 6503
Moondarra 3825
Moondooner 4605
Moondyne 6567
Moonee Beach 2450
Moonee Ponds 3039
Mooney Mooney 2083
Moongan 4714
Moonie 4406
Moonies Hill 6320
Moonta 5558
Moonyoonooka 6532
Moora 3612

Moora 6510
Moorabbin 3189
Moorabbin Airport 3194
Moorabool 3221
Moorak 5291
Mooral Creek 2429
Moore 4306
Moore Park Beach 4670
Moore River National
    Park 6503
Moorebank 1875
Moorebank 2170
Moores Pocket 4305
Mooriary 6522
Moorina 7264
Moorine Rock 6425
Moorland 2443
Moorland 4670
Moorlands 5301
Moorleah 7325
Mooroobool 4870
Moorooduc 3933
Moorook 5332
Moorooka 4105
Mooroolbark 3138
Mooroopna 3629
Moraby 4416
Moranbah 4744
Morangup 6083
Morans Crossing 2550
Morawa 6623
Morayfield 4506
Morbinning 6304
Morchard 5431
Mordalup 6258
Mordialloc 3195
Moree 2400
Moreland 3058
Morella 4730

Moresby 4871
Moresby 6530
Morgan 5320
Morgantown 6701
Morganville 4671
Moriac 3240
Moriarty 7307
Morinish 4702
Morisset 2264
Morley 6062
Morley private boxes
    6943
Morningside 4170
Mornington 3931
Mornington 4825
Mornington 6221
Mornington 7018
Morpeth 2321
Morphett Vale 5162
Morphettville 5043
Morrisons 3334
Mortdale 2223
Mortlake 2137
Mortlake 3272
Morton Vale 4343
Morundah 2700
Moruya 2537
Morven 2660
Morven 4468
Morwell 3840
Mosman 2088
Mosman Park 4820
Mosman Park 6012
Mosman Park private
    boxes 6912
Mosquito Creek 4387
Moss Vale 2577
Mossgiel 2878
Mossiface 3885

Mossman 4873
Mossy Point 2537
Motley 4356
Moulamein 2733
Moulden 0830
Moulyinning 6351
Mount Abundance 4455
Mount Adams 6525
Mount Alfred 3709
Mount Alma 4680
Mount Anketell 6714
Mount Annan 2567
Mount Archer 4514
Mount Archer 4701
Mount Austin 2650
Mount Barker 5251
Mount Barker 6324
Mount Beauty 3699
Mount Best 3960
Mount Bindango 4455
Mount Binga 4306
Mount Bryan 5418
Mount Budd 6522
Mount Buffalo 3740
Mount Buller 3723
Mount Burges 6429
Mount Burr 5279
Mount Byron 4312
Mount Carbine 4871
Mount Caroline 6410
Mount Chalmers 4702
Mount Charlton 4741
Mount Claremont 6010
Mount Clarence 6330
Mount Clear 3350
Mount Colah 2079
Mount Compass 5210
Mount Cooke 6390
Mount Coolon 4804

Mount Coolum 4573
Mount Coot-tha 4066
Mount Cotton 4165
Mount Cottrell 3024
Mount Crosby 4306
Mount Dandenong 3767
Mount David 2795
Mount Debateable 4625
Mount Delaney 4514
Mount Direction 7252
Mount Druitt 2770
Mount Duneed 3216
Mount Egerton 3345
Mount Eliza 3930
Mount Elphinstone 6330
Mount Emlyn 4357
Mount Enniskillen
Mount Erin 6532
Mount Evelyn 3796
Mount Field 7140
Mount Fox 4850
Mount Gambier 5290
Mount Gambier private
    bags 5291
Mount Gardiner 4705
Mount Garnet 4872
Mount George 2424
Mount George 5155
Mount Glorious 4520
Mount Gravatt 4122
Mount Hampton 6426
Mount Hardey 6302
Mount Hawthorn 6016
Mount Hawthorn private
    boxes 6915
Mount Helen 3350
Mount Helena 6082
Mount Hicks 7325
Mount Hill 6528

Mount Holland 6426
Mount Hope 2877
Mount Horeb 2729
Mount Horner 6525
Mount Hotham 3741
Mount Hunter 2570
Mount Hutton 2290
Mount Hutton 4454
Mount Irvine 2786
Mount Irving 4401
Mount Isa 4825
Mount Jackson 6426
Mount Jukes 4740
Mount Keira 2500
Mount Kelly 4807
Mount Kembla 2526
Mount Kuring-Gai 2080
Mount Kynoch 4350
Mount Larcom 4695
Mount Lawless 4625
Mount Lawley 6050
Mount Lawley private
   boxes 6929
Mount Lewis 2190
Mount Lewis 2200
Mount Lindesay 6333
Mount Lloyd 7140
Mount Lofty 4350
Mount Lonarch 3468
Mount Louisa 4814
Mount Luke 4352
Mount Macedon 3441
Mount Madden 6356
Mount Magnet 6638
Mount Maria 4674
Mount Marshall 4362
Mount Martha 3934
Mount Martin 4654
Mount McEuen 4606

Mount Mee 4521
Mount Melville 6330
Mount Molar 4361
Mount Molloy 4871
Mount Morgan 4714
Mount Moriac 3240
Mount Moriah 4403
Mount Mort 4340
Mount Nasura 6112
Mount Nathan 4211
Mount Nebo 4520
Mount Nelson 7007
Mount Ney 6447
Mount Observation 6302
Mount Olive 2330
Mount Ommaney 4074
Mount Osmond 5064
Mount Ossa 4741
Mount Ousley 2519
Mount Palmer 6426
Mount Pelion 4741
Mount Perry 4671
Mount Peter 4869
Mount Pleasant 2519
Mount Pleasant 3350
Mount Pleasant 4521
Mount Pleasant 4740
Mount Pleasant 5235
Mount Pleasant 6153
Mount Pluto 4800
Mount Pritchard 2170
Mount Rascal 4350
Mount Richon 6112
Mount Riverview 2774
Mount Romance 6333
Mount Rooper 4802
Mount Rowan 3352
Mount Rumney 7170
Mount Russell 2360

Mount St Thomas 2500
Mount Samson 4520
Mount Seymour 7120
Mount Sheila 6751
Mount Sheridan 4868
Mount Sheridan 6355
Mount St John 4818
Mount Stanley 4306
Mount Steadman 4650
Mount Stirling 6383
Mount Stromlo 2611
Mount Stuart 7000
Mount Surprise 4871
Mount Surround 4809
Mount Sylvia 4343
Mount Tamborine 4272
Mount Tarcoola 6530
Mount Taylor 3875
Mount Tom 4677
Mount Torrens 5244
Mount Tyson 4356
Mount Urah 4650
Mount Vernon 2178
Mount Victoria 2786
Mount View 2325
Mount Vincent 2323
Mount Walker 6369
Mount Walker West
   4340
Mount Wallace 3342
Mount Warren Park 4207
Mount Warrigal 2528
Mount Waverley 3149
Mount Wells 6390
Mount White 2250
Mount Whitestone 4347
Mount Wilson 2786
Mountain Wyatt 4804
Mountain Creek 4557

Mountain Gate 3156
Mountain River 7109
Moura 4718
Mourilyan 4858
Mouroubra 6472
Mourquong 2648
Moutajup 3294
Mowbray 7248
Moy Pocket 4574
Moyhu 3732
Moyston 3377
MP Creek 4606
MT Britton 4742
Muchea 6501
Muckadilla 4461
Muckenburra 6503
Muckleford 3451
Muckleford South 3462
Mudgee 2850
Mudgeeraba 4213
Mudgegonga 3737
Mudjimba 4564
Mudlo 4600
Mueller Ranges 6770
Muirlea 4306
Muja 6225
Mukinbudin 6479
Mulambin 4703
Mulara 4703
Mulataga 6714
Mulbring 2323
Muldu 4401
Mulga Downs 6751
Mulgildie 4630
Mulgoa 2745
Mulgrave 2756
Mulgrave 3170
Mulgrave 4807
Mullaley 2379

Mullaloo 6027
Mullalyup 6252
Mullengandra 2644
Mullengudgery 2825
Mullett Creek 4670
Mullewa 6630
Mullingar 6430
Mullion Creek 2800
Mullumbimby 2482
Muluckine 6401
Mulwala 2647
Mumballup 6225
Mumberkine 6401
Mumbil 2820
Mumbulla Mountain
   2550
Munbura 4740
Mundabullangana 6721
Mundaring 6073
Mundijong 6123
Mundingburra 4812
Mundoo 4564
Mundoora 5555
Mundowran 4626
Mundrabilla 6443
Mundubbera 4626
Mundulla 5270
Mungabunda 4718
Mungallala 4467
Mungalup 6225
Mungar 4650
Mungindi 2406
Munglinup 6450
Mungy 4671
Muniganeen 4352
Munna Creek 4570
Munno Para 5115
Munruben 4125
Munster 6166

Muntadgin 6420
Muradup 6394
Murarrie 4172
Murchison 3610
Murchison 6630
Murdinga 5607
Murdoch 6150
Murdong 6317
Murdunna 7178
Muresk 6401
Murga 2864
Murgheboluc 3221
Murgon 4605
Murmungee 3747
Murphys Creek 3551
Murphys Creek 4352
Murrabit 3579
Murrami 2705
Murray 4814
Murray Bridge 5253
Murray Bridge private
  bags 5254
Murray Town 5481
Murray Upper 4854
Murrayville 3512
Murrindindi 3717
Murringo 2586
Murroon 3243
Murrumba Downs 4503
Murrumbateman 2582
Murrumbeena 3163
Murrumburrah 2587
Murrurundi 2338
Murtoa 3390
Murwillumbah 2484
Muscle Creek 2333
Musk 3461
Musselroe Bay 7264
Muswellbrook 2333

Mutarnee 4816
Mutchilba 4872
Muttaburra 4732
Muttama 2722
Myall Park 4415
Myalla 7325
Myalup 6220
Myara 6207
Myaree 6154
Myers Flat 3556
Mylestom 2454
Mylor 5153
Myola 2540
Mypolonga 5254
Myponga 5202
Myrniong 3341
Myrtle Bank 5064
Myrtle Bank 7259
Myrtlebank 3851
Myrtleford 3737
Myrtleford private boxes
  3736
Myrtylevale 4800
Myrup 6450
Mysia 3536
Mysterton 4812

N

Nabageena 7330
Nabawa 6532
Nabiac 2312
Nabowla 7254
Nagambie 3608
Nahrunda 4570
Nailsworth 5083
Nain 5360
Nairibin 6350
Nairne 5252
Nakara 0810

Nalangil 3249
Nalkain 6485
Nalyappa 5558
Nalyerlup 6338
Namban 6512
Nambeelup 6207
Nambour 4560
Nambrok 3847
Nambucca Heads 2448
Nambung 6521
Nana Glen 2450
Nanango 4615
Nanarup 6330
Nandaly 3533
Nanga 6537
Nanga Brook 6215
Nangeenan 6414
Nangetty 6522
Nangiloc 3494
Nangrum 4416
Nangus 2722
Nangwarry 5277
Nangwee 4407
Nankin 4701
Nanneella 3561
Nannup 6275
Nanson 6532
Nanum 4874
Nanutarra 6751
Napier 6330
Napoleons 3352
Nar Nar Goon 3812
Naracoorte 5271
Naradhan 2669
Naraling 6532
Narangba 4504
Narara 2250
Narbethong 3778
Nareen 3315

Narellan 2567
Narembeen 6369
Naremburn 2065
Nariel Valley 3707
Naringal 3277
Narko 4352
Narngulu 6532
Narooma 2546
Narra Tarra 6532
Narrabeen 2101
Narrabri 2390
Narrabundah 2604
Narraloggan 6302
Narrandera 2700
Narrapumelap South
  3293
Narraweena 2099
Narrawong 3285
Narre Warren 3805
Narre Warren East 3804
Narre Warren North
  3804
Narrikup 6326
Narrogin 6312
Narromine 2821
Narrung 5259
Narwee 2209
Nashdale 2800
Nashua 2479
Nathalia 3638
Nathan 4111
Natimuk 3409
National Park 7140
Natone 7321
Nattai 2570
Natte Yallock 3465
Natural Bridge 4211
Naturaliste 6281
Naughtons Gap 2470

Naval Base 6165
Navarre 3384
Navigators 3352
Neale 6440
Nearum 4671
Nebine 4488
Nebo 4742
Nedlands 6009
Nedlands 6907
Nedlands private boxes
  6909
Needilup 6336
Needles 7304
Neendaling 6353
Neerabup 6031
Neergabby 6503
Neerim 3831
Neerim Junction 3832
Neika 7054
Neilrex 2831
Nelia 4816
Nelligen 2536
Nelly Bay 4819
Nelson 2550
Nelson 2765
Nelson 3292
Nelson Bay 2315
Nelsons Plains 2324
Nelungaloo 2876
Nembudding 5485
Nemingha 2340
Nerada 4860
Nerang 4211
Neridup 6450
Nerong 2423
Nerramyne 6630
Nerrena 3953
Nerriga 2622
Nerrigundah 2545

Nerrin Nerrin 3351
Nerrina 3350
Netherby 4650
Netherby 5062
Nethercote 2549
Netherdale 4756
Netley 5037
Neuarpurr 3413
Neumgna 4614
Neurea 2820
Neusa Vale 4570
Neutral Bay 2089
Nevertire 2831
Neville 2799
Nevilton 4361
New Auckland 4680
New Berrima 2577
New Brighton 2483
New Chum 4303
New England 2348
New Farm 4005
New Gisborne 3438
New Harbourline 4858
New Lambton 2305
New Moonta 4671
New Norcia 6509
New Norfolk 7140
New Town 5554
New Town 7008
New Well 5357
Newborough 3825
Newbridge 2795
Newbridge 3551
Newbury 3458
Newcarlbeon 6475
Newcastle 2300
Newcastle East 2300
Newcastle University
  2308

Newcastle Waters 0862
Newcastle West 2302
Newcomb 3219
Newdegate 6355
Newel 4873
Newham 3442
Newhaven 3925
Newington 2127
Newlands 4804
Newlands 6251
Newlands Arm 3875
Newlyn 3364
Newman 6753
Newmarket 4051
Newmerella 3886
Newnham 7248
Newport 2106
Newport 3015
Newport Beach 2106
Newry 3859
Newstead 3462
Newstead 4006
Newstead 7250
Newton 5074
Newton Boyd 2370
Newtown 2042
Newtown 3220
Newtown 4305
Newtown 4350
Nguiu 0822
Ngukurr 0852
Ngunnawal 2913
Nhill 3418
Nhulunbuy 0880
Nhulunbuy private boxes
  0881
Niagara Park 2250
Niangala 2354
Nicholls 2913

Nicholls Rivulet 7112
Nichols Point 3501
Nicholson 3882
Nickol 6714
Niddrie 3042
Nietta 7315
Nightcliff 0810
Nightcliff private boxes
  0814
Nikenbah 4655
Nildottie 5238
Nile 7212
Nilgen 6044
Nillup 6288
Nilma 3821
Nimbin 2480
Nimmitabel 2631
Nindaroo 4740
Nine Mile 4702
Nine Mile Creek 4714
Ningaloo 6701
Ningi 4511
Nippering 6350
Nirimba 6208
Nirranda 3268
Njatjan 4860
Noarlunga Centre 5168
Noarlunga Downs 5168
Nobby 4360
Nobby Beach 4218
Noble Park 3174
Noggerup 6225
Nokaning 6415
Nolba 6532
Nollamara 6061
Nomans Lake 6312
Nome 4816
Nonning 5710
Noojee 3833

Nook 7306
Noonamah 0837
Noonbinna 2794
Noorama 4490
Noorat 3265
Noorinbee 3890
Noosa Heads 4567
Noosaville 4566
Noradjuha 3409
Norah Head 2263
Noranda 6062
Noraville 2263
Nords Wharf 2281
Norfolk Island 2899
Norlane 3214
Norman Gardens 4701
Norman Park 4170
Normanhurst 2076
Normanton 4890
Normanville 5204
Nornalup 6333
Norong 3682
Norpa 6415
Norseman 6443
North Adelaide 5006
North Albury 2640
North Aramara 4620
North Arm Cove 2324
North Avoca 2260
North Baandee 4218
North Bannister 6390
North Batemans Bay
  2536
North Beach 6020
North Beach private
  boxes 6920
North Bendigo 3550
North Bodallin 6424
North Booval 4304

North Boyanup 6237
North Branch 4356
North Bungunya 4494
North Burngup 6353
North Cascade 6445
North Coogee 6163
North Curl Curl 2099
North Dandalup 6207
North Deep Creek 4570
North Eradu 6532
North Fremantle 6159
North Geelong 3215
North Greenbushes 6254
North Gregory 4660
North Haven 2443
North Haven 5018
North Hobart 7000
North Hobart private
  boxes 7002
North Ipswich 4305
North Jindong 6280
North Kellerberrin 6410
North Kukerin 6352
North Kununoppin 6489
North Lake 6163
North Lake Grace 6353
North Lakes 4509
North Lambton 2299
North Lilydale 7628
North Lismore 2480
North Mackay 4740
North MacLagan 4352
North Maleny 4552
North Manly 2100
North Melbourne 3051
North Moonta 5558
North Motton 7315
North Moulyinning 6351
North Narooma 2546

North Nowra 2541
North Parramatta 1750
North Parramatta 2151
North Perth 6006
North Perth private
  boxes 6906
North Plantations 6701
North Plympton 5037
North Richmond 2754
North Road 3187
North Rockhampton
  4701
North Rocks 2151
North Rothbury 2335
North Ryde 2113
North Shore 3214
North Shore 4565
North Star 2408
North Stirlings 6338
North Stathfield 2137
North Sydney 2060
North Sydney private
  boxes 2059
North Talwood 4496
North Tamborine 4272
North Tivoli 4305
North Toowoomba 4350
North Trayning 6488
North Turramurra 2074
North Walpole 6398
North Ward 4810
North Warrandyte 3113
North West Cape 6707
North Wialki 6473
North Willoughby 2068
North Wollongong 2500
North Yelbeni 6487
North Yelta 5558
North Yunderup 6208

Northam 6401
Northampton 6535
Northbridge 1560
Northbridge 2063
Northbridge 6003
Northbridge private
  boxes 6865
Northcliffe 6262
Northcote 3070
Northdown 7307
Northern Gully 6532
Northfield 5085
Northgate 4013
Northgate 5085
Northland Centre 3072
Northlands 4350
Northlands 6905
Northmead 2152
Northwood 2066
Norton Summit 5136
Norville 4670
Norwell 4208
Norwin 4356
Norwood 5067
Norwood 7250
Notley Hills 7275
Notting Hill 3168
Novar Gardens 5040
Nowa Nowa 3887
Nowerdoc 2354
Nowergup 6032
Nowra 2541
Nubeena 7184
Nudgee 4014
Nugadong 6609
Nugent 7172
Nukarni 6480
Nukku 4306
Nulkaba 2325

Nullagine 6758
Nullaki 6330
Nullamanna 2360
Nullawarre 3268
Nullawil 3529
Nulsen 6450
Numbaa 2540
Number One 2424
Numbla Vale 2628
Numbulwar 0852
Numeralla 2630
Numinbah 2484
Numinbah Valley 4711
Numulgi 2480
Numurkah 3636
Nunamara 7259
Nunawading 3131
Nundah 4012
Nundle 2340
Nungarin 6490
Nunierra 6630
Nunile 6566
Nuriootpa 5355
Nutfield 3099
Nyabing 6341
Nyah 3594
Nyah West 3595
Nyirripi 0872
Nymagee 2831
Nymboida 2460
Nyngan 2825
Nyora 3987

O

O.B. Flat 5291
Oak Flats 2529
Oak Park 3046
Oak Valley 4811
Oakajee 6532

Oakbank 5243
Oakdale 2570
Oakdale 4605
Oakden 5086
Oakey 4401
Oakey Creek 4714
Oakford 6113
Oakhurst 2761
Oakhurst 4650
Oaklands 2646
Oaklands Junction 3063
Oaklands Park 5046
Oakleigh 3166
Oakleigh South 3167
Oakley 6208
Oakview 4600
Oakville 2765
Oatlands 2117
Oatlands 7120
Oatley 2223
Oberon 2787
O'Briens Hill 4860
Ocean Beach 6333
Ocean Grove 3226
Ocean Reef 6027
Ocean Shores 2483
Ocean View 4521
O'Connell 4680
O'Connor 2602
O'Connor 6163
Oenpelli 0822
Officer 3809
Ogilvie 6535
Ogmore 4706
O'Halloran Hill 5158
Okeden 4613
Olary 5440
Old Bar 2430
Old Beach 7017

Old Bonalbo 2469
Old Cooranga 2626
Old Erowal Bay 2540
Old Guildford 2161
Old Junee 2652
Old Koreelah 2476
Old Noarlunga 5168
Old Plains 6569
Old Toongabbie 2146
Oldbury 6121
Oldina 7325
Olinda 3788
Olympic Dam 5725
O'Malley 2606
Oman Ama 4352
Omeo 3898
Ondit 3249
One Mile 4305
One Tree Hill 5114
Ongerup 6336
Onkaparinga Hills 5163
Onslow 6710
Oodnadatta 5734
Oombabeer 4718
Oombulgurri 6740
Oonoonba 4811
Ooralea 4740
Oorindi 4824
Ootha 2797
Opalton 4735
Opossum Bay 7023
Opossum Creek 2479
Ora Banda 6431
Orallo 4455
Orana 6330
Orange 2800
Orange Creek 4715
Orange Grove 2380
Orange Grove 6109

Orange Hill 4455
Orange Springs 6503
Orangeville 2570
Orbost 3888
Orchard Hills 2748
Orchid Valley 6394
Ord River 6770
Orelia 6167
Orford 7190
Orielton 7172
Orient Point 2540
Ormeau 4208
Ormiston 4160
Ormond 3204
Ororroo 5431
Osborne 4806
Osborne 5017
Osborne Park 6017
Osborne Park private
  boxes 700-762 6916
Osborne Park private
  boxes 1001-1515 6916
Osborne Park private
  boxes 1-515 6917
Osmington 6285
Osterley 2324
Osterley 7140
O'Sullivan Beach 5166
Otago 7017
Otford 2508
Ottaba 4313
Ottoway 5013
Ourimbah 2258
Ouse 7140
Outer Harbor 5018
Outtrim 3951
Ouyen 3490
Ovens 3738
Ovingham 5082

Owanyilla 4650
Owen 5460
Owens Creek 4741
Owens Gap 2337
Oxenford 4210
Oxford 4742
Oxford Falls 2100
Oxley 2711
Oxley 2903
Oxley 3678
Oxley 4075
Oxley Park 2760
Oxley Vale 2340
Oyster Bay 2225
Oyster 2318
Oyster Cove 7150
Oyster Creek 4674
Ozenkadnook 3413

P

Pacific Fair 4218
Pacific Haven 4659
Pacific Heights 4703
Pacific Palms 2428
Pacific Paradise 4564
Pacific pines 4211
Padbury 6025
Paddington 2021
Paddington 4064
Padstow 2211
Padthaway 5271
Page 2614
Paget 4740
Pagewood 2035
Painswick 3551
Pakenham 3810
Palana 7255
Palen Creek 4287
Palgarup 6258

Palinyewah 2648
Pallamallawa 2399
Pallara 4110
Pallarenda 4810
Pallinup 6335
Palm Beach 2108
Palm Beach 4221
Palm Cove 4879
Palm Grove 4800
Palm Island 4816
Palmdale 6328
Palmer 5237
Palmer 6225
Palmerston 0830
Palmerston private
  boxes 0831
Palmerston 2913
Palmerston 4860
Palmtree 4352
Palmvale 2484
Palmview 4553
Palmwoods 4555
Palmyra 6157
Palmyra private boxes
  6957
Paloona 7310
Paluma 4816
Pambula 2549
Pampas 4352
Panania 2213
Panmure 3265
Pannawonica 6716
Panorama 5041
Pantapin 6384
Panton Hill 3759
Pappinbarra 2446
Papunya 0872
Para Hills 5096
Para Vista 5093

Paraburdoo 6754
Parachilna 5730
Paracombe 5132
Paradise 5075
Paradise 6236
Paradise 7306
Paradise Beach 3851
Paradise Point 4216
Parafield 5106
Parafield Gardens 5107
Paralowie 5108
Parap private boxes 0804
Parattah 7120
Pardoo 6721
Parilla 5303
Paringa 5340
Paringi 3500
Park Avenue 4701
Park Holme 5043
Park Orchards 3114
Park Ridge 4125
Parkdale 3195
Parker Range 6426
Parkerville 6081
Parkes 2600
Parkes 2870
Parkeston 6434
Parkfield 6233
Parkham 7304
Parkhurst 4702
Parkinson 4115
Parklands 6210
Parklea 2768
Parkside 4807
Parkside 4825
Parkside 5063
Parkville 2337
Parkville 3052

Parkwood 4214
Parkwood 6147
Parliament House
  Canberra 2600
Parmelia 6167
Parndana 5220
Parrakie 5301
Parramatta
  Commonwealth
  Offices 2123
Parramatta private
  boxes 2124
Parramatta 2150
Parramatta Park 4870
Parrawe 7321
Parrearra 4575
Parryville 6333
Paruna 5311
Parwan 3340
Pasadena 5042
Pascoe Vale 3044
Pasha 4721
Paskeville 5552
Patchewollock 3491
Paterson 2421
Paterson 4570
Patersonia 7259
Patho 3564
Patonga 2256
Patrick Estate 4311
Patterson Lakes 3197
Paulls Valley 6076
Pauls Pocket 4800
Pawleena 7172
Pawtella 7120
Paxton 2325
Paynedale 6239
Payneham 5070
Paynes Crossing 2325

Point Clare 2250
Point Cook 3030
Point Grey 6208
Point Lonsdale 3225
Point Lookout 4183
Point McLeay 5259
Point Pearce 5573
Point Piper 2027
Point Samson 6720
Point Turton 5575
Point Vernon 4655
Pokolbin 2320
Police Point 7116
Pomborneit 3260
Pomona 2648
Pomona 4568
Pomonal 3381
Pontville 7030
Pony Hills 4454
Poochera 5655
Poolaijelo 3312
Pooncarie 2648
Pooraka 5095
Pootilla 3352
Poowong 3988
Popanyinning 6309
Porepunkah 3740
Porongurup 6324
Port Adelaide 5015
Port Albany 6330
Port Albert 3971
Port Alma 4699
Port Arthur 7182
Port Augusta 5700
Port Augusta private
 bags 5710
Port Botany 2036
Port Broughton 5522

Port Campbell 3269
Port Clinton 5555
Port Curtis 4700
Port Denison 6525
Port Douglas 4877
Port Elliot 5212
Port Fairy 3284
Port Flinders 5495
Port Franklin 3964
Port Gawler 5501
Port Germein 5495
Port Hacking 2229
Port Hedland 6721
Port Hughes 5558
Port Huon 7116
Port Kembla 2505
Port Kennedy 6172
Port Kenny 5671
Port Lincoln 5606
Port Lincoln private bags
 5607
Port MacDonnell 5291
Port Macquarie 2444
Port Melbourne 3207
Port Neill 5604
Port Noarlunga 5167
Port of Brisbane 4178
Port Pirie 5540
Port Rickaby 5575
Port Sorell 7307
Port Victoria 5573
Port Vincent 5581
Port Wakefield 5550
Port Welshpool 3965
Port Willunga 5173
Portarlington 3223
Porters Retreat 2787
Portland 2847
Portland 3305

Portsea 3944
Postans 6167
Postmans Ridge 4352
Potts Hill 2143
Potts Point 1335
Potts Point 2011
Pottsville 2489
Powelltown 3797
Powranna 7300
Pozieres 4352
Prahran 3181
Prairie 3572
Prairie 4816
Prairiewood 2176
Premaydena 7185
Premer 2381
Prentice North 3685
Preolenna 7325
Preservation Bay 7316
Preston 3072
Preston 4352
Preston 4800
Preston 7315
Preston Beach 6215
Preston Settlement 6225
Prestons 2170
Pretty Beach 2257
Prevelly 6285
Price 5570
Priestdale 4127
Primbee 2502
Primrose Sands 7173
Prince Henry Heights
 4350
Prince Regent River 6740
Princetown 3269
Promisedland 4660
Proserpine 4800
Prospect 2148

Prospect 4715
Prospect 5082
Prospect 7250
Prospect Hill 5201
Prospect Vale 7250
Proston 4613
Puckapunyal 3662
Pularumpi 0822
Pullabooka 2810
Pullenvale 4069
Pumphreys Bridge 6308
Punchbowl 2196
Punchbowl 7249
Punchs Creek 4357
Pura Pura 3271
Purfleet 2430
Purlewaugh 2357
Purnim 3278
Purnululu 6770
Purrawunda 4356
Putney 2112
Putty 2330
Pyalong 3521
Pyengana 7216
Pymble 2073
Pyramid Hill 3575
Pyree 2540
Pyrmont 2009

Q

Quaama 2550
Quairading 6383
Quakers Hill 2763
Qualeup 6394
Quambatook 3540
Quambone 2831
Quandialla 2721
Quantong 3401
Quarry Hill 3550

Queanbeyan 2620
Quedjinup 6281
Queen Victoria Building
 1230
Queens Beach 4805
Queens Park 2022
Queens Park 6107
Queenscliff 2096
Queenscliff 3225
Queenstown 5014
Queenstown 7467
Queenton 4820
Queenwood 6239
Quelagetting 6405
Quellington 6302
Quilpie 4480
Quinalow 4403
Quindalup 6281
Quindanning 6391
Quinninup 6258
Quinns Rocks 6030
Quirindi 2343
Qunaba 4670
Quoiba 7310
Quorn 5433
Quorrobolong 2325

R

Raby 2566
Racecourse 4740
Raceview 4305
Raglan 2795
Raglan 4697
Ralton 7305
Railway Estate 4810
Rainbow 3424
Rainbow Beach 4581
Raleigh 2454
Ramco 5322

Raminea 7109
Ramingining 0822
Ramsay 4352
Ramsgate 2217
Rand 2642
Randalls Bay 7112
Randwick 2031
Ranelagh 7109
Ranford 6390
Ranga 7255
Rangemore 4352
Rangemore 4806
Rangeview 3132
Rangeville 4350
Rangeway 6530
Rankin Park 2287
Rankins Springs 2669
Ransome 4154
Rapid Bay 5204
Rapid Creek 0810
Rappville 2469
Rasmussen 4815
Rathdowney 4287
Rathmines 2283
Rathscar 3465
Raukkan 5259
Ravensbourne 4352
Ravensdale 2259
Ravenshoe 4872
Ravensthorpe 6346
Ravenswood 3453
Ravenswood 4816
Ravenswood 6208
Ravenswood 7250
Ravensworlh 2330
Rawdon Vale 2422
Rawlinna 6434
Raworth 2321
Rawson 3825

Raymond Island 3880
Raymond Terrace 2324
Raywood 3570
Razorback 2571
Red Bluff 3695
Red Cliffs 3496
Red Gully 6503
Red Hill 2603
Red Hill 3937
Red Hill 4059
Red Hill 6056
Red Hills 7304
Red Range 2370
Red Rock 2456
Redan 3350
Redbank 3478
Redbank 4301
Redbank 6721
Redbank Creek 4312
Redcliffe 4020
Redcliffe 6104
Redesdale 3444
Redfern 2016
Redgate 4605
Redgate 6286
Redhead 2290
Redhill 5521
Redhill Farms 4671
Redland Bay 4165
Redlynch 4870
Redmond 6327
Redpa 7330
Redwood 4350
Redwood Park 5097
Reedy 6640
Reedy Creek 2330
Reedy Creek 3658
Reedy Creek 4227
Reedy Marsh 7304

Reefton 2666
Reeves Plains 5502
Regans Ford 6507
Regency Park 5010
Regency Park private
  boxes 5942
Regent West 3072
Regents Park 2143
Regents Park 4118
Regentville 2745
Reid 2612
Reids Creek 4625
Reids Flat 2586
Reidsdale 2622
Reinscourt 6280
Relbia 7258
Remlap 6472
Rendelsham 5280
Renison Bell 7469
Renmark 5341
Rennie 2646
Renown Park 5008
Repton 2454
Research 3095
Reservoir 3073
Reservoir 6076
Retreat 7254
Revesby 2212
Reynella 5161
Rhodes 2138
Rhydding 4718
Rhyll 3923
Rhyndaston 7120
Riana 7316
Richardson 2905
Richlands 4077
Richmond 2753
Richmond 3121
Richmond 4740

Richmond 4822
Richmond 5033
Richmond 7025
Richmond Hill 2480
Richmond Hill 4820
Richmond RAAF 2755
Riddells Creek 3431
Ridgehaven 5097
Ridgelands 4702
Ridgeway 2620
Ridgeway 7054
Ridgewood 6030
Ridgley 7321
Ridleyton 5008
Rileys Hill 2472
Ringarooma 7263
Ringbark 6258
Ringtail Creek 4565
Ringwood 3134
Ringwood 4343
Ringwood East 3135
Ripley 4306
Ripplebrook 3818
Ripponlea 3185
Risdon Park 5540
Risdon Vale 7016
Rite Island 4807
River Ranch 4680
Riverhills 4074
Riverleigh 4626
Riverside 3401
Riverside 7250
Riverside Centre private
  boxes 4001
Riverstone 2765
Riverton 4385
Riverton 5412
Riverton 6148
Rivervale 6103

Riverview 2066
Riverview 4303
Riverwood 2210
Rivett 2611
Roadvale 4310
Robe 5276
Robertson 2577
Robertson 4109
Robertstown 5381
Robigana 7275
Robina 4226
Robina Town Centre
  4230
Robinson 3019
Robinson 6330
Robinvale 3549
Rochedale 4123
Rocherlea 7248
Roches Beach 7021
Rochester 3561
Rochford 3442
Rock Rat 2630
Rock Valley 2480
Rockbank 3335
Rockdale 2216
Rockhampton 4700
Rockingham 6168
Rockingham 6968
Rockingham Beach 6969
Rocklands 3401
Rocklea 4106
Rocklea 6751
Rockley 2795
Rocklyn 3364
Rockmount 4344
Rockside 4343
Rockville 4350
Rockwell 6532
Rocky Cape 7321

Rocky Creek 4357
Rocky Glen 2357
Rocky Gully 6397
Rocky Hall 2550
Rocky Point 4874
Rockyview 4701
Rodd Point 2046
Rodds Bay 4678
Roebourne 6718
Roebuck 6725
Roelands 6226
Rokeby 3821
Rokeby 7019
Rokewood 3330
Rokewood Junction 3351
Roland 7306
Roleystone 6111
Rollands Plains 2441
Rolleston 4702
Rollingstone 4816
Roma 4455
Romaine 7320
Romsey 3434
Rooty Hill 2766
Ropeley 4343
Rosa Brook 6285
Rosa Glen 6285
Rosalie Plains 4401
Rosanna 3084
Rose Bay 2029
Rose Bay 7015
Rose Bay North 2030
Rose Park 5067
Rose Valley 2630
Rosebank 2480
Rosebery 0832
Rosebery 1445
Rosebery 2018
Rosebery 7470

Rosebrook 3285
Rosebud 3939
Rosebud West 3940
Rosedale 2536
Rosedale 3847
Rosedale 4674
Rosegarland 7140
Rosehill 2142
Roselands 2196
Rosella 4740
Rosemeadow 2560
Roseneath 4811
Rosetta 7010
Rosevale 7292
Rosevears 7277
Roseville 2069
Rosewater 5013
Rosewood 2652
Rosewood 4340
Roseworthy 5371
Roslyn 2580
Rosny 7018
Ross 7209
Ross Creek 3351
Ross Creek 4570
Ross River 4816
Rossarden 7213
Rosslea 4812
Rosslyn 4703
Rosslyn Park 5072
Rossmore 2171
Rossmore 6401
Rossmoya 4702
Rossmoyne 6148
Rossvale 4356
Rostrevor 5073
Rothbury 2320
Rothsay 6620
Rothwell 4022

Roto 2675
Rottnest Island 6161
Rouchel 2336
Round Corner 2158
Round Hill 4677
Roundstone 4718
Rous 2477
Rous Mill 2477
Rouse Hill 2155
Rowella 7270
Rowena 2387
Rowes Bay 4810
Rowland Flat 5352
Rowsley 3340
Rowville 3178
Roxburgh Park 3064
Roxby Downs 5725
Royal Australian Navy
   Warships Perth 6958
Royal Brisbane Hospital
   4029
Royal Exchange 1225
Royal George 7213
Royal Melbourne
   Hospital 3050
Royal North Shore
   Hospital 2065
Royal Park 5014
Royalla 2620
Royston Park 5070
Rozelle 2039
Ruabon 6280
Rubicon 3712
Rubyanna 4670
Rubyvale 4702
Rudall 5642
Rudds Gully 6532
Ruffy 3666
Rufus River 2648

Rugby 2583
Rukervale 2474
Rules Beach 4674
Runaway Bay 4216
Runcorn 4113
Running Stream 2850
Runnyford 2536
Runnymede 4615
Runnymede 7190
Rupanyup 3388
Rural View 4740
Ruse 2560
Rush Creek 4521
Rushcutters Bay 2011
Rushworlh 3612
Russell 2600
Russell Island 4184
Russell Lea 2046
Russell Vale 2517
Russells Bridge 3331
Rutherford 2320
Rutherglen 3685
Ruthven 2480
Ryan 2658
Ryan 4825
Ryansbrook 6395
Rydal 2790
Rydalmere 2116
Ryde 1680
Ryde 2112
Rye 3941
Rye Park 2586
Ryeford 4361
Rylstone 2849

S
Saddleworth 5413
Sadleir 2168
Sadliers Crossing 4305

Safety Bay 6169
Safety Beach 2456
Safety Beach 3936
Saint Helena 3088
Salamander Bay 2301
Sale 3850
Sale private boxes 3853
Salisbury 2420
Salisbury 4107
Salisbury 5108
Salisbury Downs 5108
Salisbury East 5109
Salisbury Heights 5109
Salisbury North 5108
Salisbury Park 5109
Salisbury Plain 5109
Salisbury South 5106
Salisbury West 3517
Salmon Gums 6445
Salt Ash 2318
Salter Point 6152
Saltwater River 7186
Samford 4520
Samson 6163
Samsonvale 4520
San Remo 2262
San Remo 3925
San Remo 6210
Sanctuary Cove 4212
Sanctuary Point 2540
Sandalwood 5309
Sanderson 0812
Sanderson private boxes
   0813
Sanderston 5237
Sandfly 7150
Sandford 3312
Sandford 7020
Sandgate 2304

Sandgate 4017
Sandhurst 3977
Sandhurst East 3550
Sandiford 4740
Sandown Village 3171
Sandpatch 6330
Sandringham 2219
Sandringham 3191
Sandringham 4701
Sandsprings 6532
Sandstone 6639
Sandstone Point 4511
Sandy Bay 7005
Sandy Bay private boxes 7006
Sandy Beach 2456
Sandy Camp 4361
Sandy Creek 3695
Sandy Creek 5350
Sandy Flat 2372
Sandy Gully 6535
Sandy Hollow 2333
Sandy Pocket 4871
Sandy Point 2171
Sandy Point 3959
Sandy Ridges 4615
Sans Souci 2219
Santa Teresa 0872
Sapphire 4702
Saratoga 2251
Sarina 4737
Sarsfield 3875
Sassafras 3787
Sassafras 7307
Satur 2337
Saunders Beach 4816
Savage River 7321
Savernake 2646
Sawtell 2452

Sawyers Valley 6074
Scadden 6447
Scamander 7215
Scarborough 2515
Scarborough 4020
Scarborough 6019
Scarborough 6922
Scarness 4655
Scarsdale 3351
Scheyville 2756
Schofields 2762
Schroeder 6285
Scone 2337
Scoresby 3179
Scotchy Pocket 4570
Scotland Island 2105
Scotsburn 3352
Scotsdale 6333
Scott Creek 5153
Scott River 6288
Scott River East 6275
Scotts Brook 6244
Scotts Creek 3267
Scotts Head 2447
Scottsdale 7260
Scrub Creek 4313
Scrubby Creek 4478
Scrubby Creek 4570
Scrubby Mountain 4356
Scullin 2614
Sea Lake 3533
Seabird 6042
Seabrook 3028
Seacliff 5049
Seacliff Park 5049
Seacombe Gardens 5047
Seacombe Heights 5047
Seaford 3198
Seaford 5169

Seaforth 2092
Seaforth 4741
Seaham 2324
Seaholme 3018
Seal Rocks 2423
Seaspray 3851
Seaton 3858
Seaton 5023
Seaview Downs 5049
Sebastian 3556
Sebastopol 2666
Sebastopol 3356
Second Valley 5204
Secret Harbour 6173
Sedan 5353
Seddon 3011
Seelands 2460
Sefton 2162
Sefton Park 5083
Selbourne 7292
Selby 3159
Selene 4630
Sellheim 4816
Sellicks Beach 5174
Sellicks Hill 5174
Semaphore 5019
Seppeltsfield 5355
Seppings 6330
Septimus 4754
Serpentine 3517
Serpentine 6125
Serviceton 3420
Seven Hills 1730
Seven Hills 2147
Seven Hills 4170
Seven Mile Beach 7170
Seventeen Mile 4344
Seventeen Mile Rocks 4073

Seventeen Seventy 4677
Severnlea 4352
Seville 3139
Seville Grove 6112
Sexton 4570
Sextonville 2470
Seymour 3660
Seymour private boxes 3661
Seymour 7215
Shacklcton 6306
Shadforth 6333
Shailer Park 4128
Shalvey 2770
Shanes Park 2747
Shannon 7030
Shannon Brook 2470
Sharon 4670
She Oaks 3331
Shea-oak Log 5371
Shearwater 7307
Sheep Hills 3392
Sheffield 7306
Sheidow Park 5158
Shelbourne 3463
Sheldon 4157
Shelford 3329
Shell Cove 2529
Shell Pocket 4855
Shelley 3701
Shelley 6148
Shellharbour 2529
Shelly Beach 2261
Shelly Beach 4551
Shelly Beach 4810
Shenton Park 6008
Shepparton 3630
Shepparton East 3631

Shepparton private boxes 3632
Sherbrooke 3789
Sherlock 5301
Sherlock 6714
Sherwood 4075
Shirbourne 4809
Shoal Bay 2315
Shoal Point 4750
Shoalhaven Heads 2535
Shoalwater 4702
Shoalwater 6169
Shooters Hill 2787
Shoreham 3916
Shorncliffe 4017
Shortland 2307
Shotts 6225
Shute Harbour 4802
Sidmouth 7270
Siesta Park 6280
Silkstone 4304
Silkwood 4856
Silkwood East 4857
Silvan 3795
Silver Creek 4800
Silver Ridge 4344
Silver Sands 6210
Silver Spur 4385
Silver Valley 4872
Silverdale 2752
Silverleaf 4605
Silverleigh 4401
Silverton 2880
Silverwater 1811
Silverwater 2128
Silverwater 2264
Simmie 3564
Simmie 4454
Simpson 3266

Simpsons Bay 7150
Simson 3465
Sinagra 6065
Sinclair 6450
Singleton 2330
Singleton 6175
Sinnamon Park 4073
Sippy Downs 4556
Sir Samuel 6437
Sisters Beach 7321
Sisters Creek 7325
Skeleton Rock 6426
Skenes Creek 3233
Skinners Flat 3518
Skipton 3361
Skye 3977
Skye 5072
Skyring Reserve 4671
Slacks Creek 4127
Slade Point 4740
Smeaton 3364
Smiggin Holes 2624
Smith Brook 6258
Smithfield 2164
Smithfield 4878
Smithfield 5114
Smithfield West 2164
Smithlea 4385
Smiths Gully 3760
Smiths Lake 2428
Smithton 7330
Smithtown 2440
Smoky Bay 5680
Smoky Creek 4702
Smythes Creek 3351
Smythesdale 3351
Snake Valley 3351
Snowtown 5520
Snug 7054

Sodwalls 2790
Sofala 2795
Soldiers Hill 4825
Soldiers Point 2317
Solomontown 5540
Solus 6207
Somers 3927
Somersby 2250
Somerset 7322
Somerset Dam 4312
Somerton 2340
Somerton 3062
Somerton Park 5044
Somerville 3912
Somerville 6430
Sorell 7172
Sorell Creek 7140
Sorrento 3943
Sorrento 6020
South Albury 2640
South Arm 2460
South Arm 7022
South Bingera 4670
South Bodallin 6424
South Boulder 6432
South Brighton 5048
South Brisbane 4101
South Bunbury 6230
South Burracoppin 6421
South Carnarvon 6701
South Datatine 6317
South Doodlakine 6411
South Dudley 3995
South Durras 2536
South East Nanango
   4615
South Fremantle 6162
South Gladstone 4680
South Glencoe 6317

South Golden Beach
   2483
South Grafton 2460
South Greenough 6528
South Guildford 6055
South Hedland 6722
South Hobart 7004
South Hurstville 2221
South Innisfail 4860
South Johnstone 4859
South Kalgoorlie 6430
South Kempsey 2440
South Kilkerran 5573
South Kingsvale 3015
South Kolan 4670
South Kukerin 6352
South Kumminin 6368
South Kununoppin 6489
South Lake 6164
South Lake Grace 6353
South Launceston 7249
South Mackay 4740
South Melbourne 3205
South Molle 4741
South Morang 3752
South Mount Cameron
   7264
South Murchison 6635
South Newdegate 6355
South Nowra 2541
South Pambula 2549
South Perth 6151
South Perth private
   boxes 6951
South Plantations 6701
South Plympton 5038
South Quairading 6383
South Riana 7316
South Ripley 4306

South Stirling 6324
South Stradbroke 4216
South Talwood 4496
South Tamworth 2340
South Toowoomba 4350
South Townsville 4810
South Trayning 6488
South Trees 4680
South Turramurra 2074
South West Rocks 2431
South Yaamba 4702
South Yarra 3141
South Yelbeni 6487
South Yilgarin 6426
South Yuna 6532
South Yunderup 6208
Southampton 6253
Southbank 3006
Southbrook 4363
Southend 5280
Southern Brook 6401
Southern Cross 3282
Southern Cross 6426
Southern River 6110
Southland Centre 3192
Southport 4215
Southport 7109
Souttlown 4350
Sovereign Hill 3350
Spalding 5454
Spalding 6530
Spalford 7315
Spearwood 6163
Speed 3488
Speers Point 2284
Spence 2615
Spencer 2775
Spencer Park 6330
Spencers Brook 6401

Spicers Creek 2820
Spit Junction 2088
Splinter Creek 4630
Spotswood 3015
Sprent 7315
Spreyton 7310
Spring Beach 7190
Spring Bluff 4352
Spring Creek 4343
Spring Creek 4361
Spring Grove 2470
Spring Gully 3550
Spring Hill 2500
Spring Hill 2800
Spring Hill 4000
Spring Hill private boxes
   4004
Spring Ridge 2343
Springbank 3352
Springbrook 4213
Springdale 2666
Springfield 2250
Springfield 4300
Springfield 5062
Springfield 6525
Springfield 7260
Springfield Lakes 4300
Springhurst 3682
Springlands 4804
Springs 6308
Springside 4356
Springsure 4722
Springton 5235
Springvale 3171
Springvale South 3172
Springwood 2777
Springwood 4127
St Agnes 4671
St Agnes 5097

St Albans 2775
St Albans 3021
St Albans Park 3219
St Andrews 2566
St Andrews 3761
St Andrews Beach 3941
St Arnaud 3478
St Aubyn 4352
St Clair 2330
St Clair 2759
St George 4487
St Georges 5064
St Georges Basin 2540
St Helens 3285
St Helens 4356
St Helens 4650
St Helens 7216
St Helens Park 2560
St Huberts Island 2257
St Ives 2075
St James 3727
St James 6102
St Johns Park 2176
St Kilda 3182
St Kilda 4671
St Kilda 5110
St Kilda East 3183
St Lawrence 4707
St Leonards 1590
St Leonards 2065
St Leonards 3223
St Leonards 7250
St Lucia 4067
St Mary 4570
St Marys 1790
St Marys 2760
St Marys 5042
St Marys 7215
St Morris 5068

St Pauls 2031
St Peters 2044
St Peters 5069
St Ronans 6302
Stafford 4053
Staghorn Flat 3691
Stake Hill 6210
Stamford 4821
Stanage 4702
Stanford Merthyr 2327
Stanhope 2335
Stanhope 3623
Stanhope Gardens 2768
Stanley 3747
Stanley 7331
Stanmore 2048
Stannifer 2369
Stannum 2371
Stansbury 5582
Stanthorpe 4380
Stanwell 4702
Stanwell Park 2508
Stanwell Tops 2508
Stapylton 4207
Station Arcade 5000
Staughton Vale 3221
Stavely 3379
Staverton 7306
Stawell 3380
Steels Creek 3775
Steiglitz 3331
Steiglitz 4207
Stenhouse Bay 5575
Stepney 5069
Steppes 7030
Stewarton 4702
Stewarts Brook 2337
Stieglitz 7216
Stirling 2611

Stirling 5152
Stirling 6021
Stirling 6271
Stirling North 5710
Stirling Range National
    Park 6338
Stockhaven 4625
Stockinbingal 2725
Stockport 5410
Stockton 2295
Stockton 4871
Stockwell 5355
Stockyard 4344
Stockyard 4703
Stokers Siding 2484
Stone Well 5352
Stonehaven 3221
Stonehenge 4357
Stonehenge 4730
Stonehenge 7120
Stonelands 4612
Stoneleigh 4356
Stones Corner 4120
Stoneville 6081
Stonor 7119
Stony Creek 3371
Stony Creek 3957
Stony Creek 4514
Stonyfell 5066
Stonyford 3260
Stoodley 7306
Stormlea 7184
Stoters Hill 4860
Stotts Creek 2487
Stove Hill 6714
Stowport 7321
Strahan 7468
Stratford 2422
Strafford 3862

Stratford 4870
Strath Creek 3658
Strathalbyn 5255
Strathalbyn 6530
Strathallan 3622
Stratham 6237
Strathblane 7109
Strathbogie 3666
Strathdale 3550
Strathdownie 3312
Strathdon 2470
Stratherne 6309
Strathewen 3099
Strathfield 2135
Strathfield 4742
Strathfield South 2136
Strathfieldsaye 3551
Strathgordon 7139
Strathkellar 3301
Strathmerton 3641
Strathmore 3041
Strathpine 4500
Stratton 6056
Strawberry Hills 2012
Streaky Bay 5680
Streatham 3351
Strelley 6721
Stretton 4116
Strickland 7140
Stroud 2425
Stroud Road 2415
Stuart 4811
Stuart Mill 3478
Stuart Park 0820
Stuart Town 2820
Stuarts Point 2441
Studfield 3152
Studio Village 4210
Sturt 4829

Sturt 5047
Sturt Creek 6770
Subiaco 6008
Subiaco private boxes
    6904
Success 6164
Success private boxes
    6964
Suffolk Park 2481
Sugarloaf 4800
Sulphur Creek 7316
Summer Hill 2130
Summerhill 2287
Summerhill 7250
Summerland Point 2259
Summertown 5141
Sumner 4074
Sun Valley 4680
Sunbury 3429
Sundown 4860
Sunny Corner 2795
Sunny Nook 4605
Sunnybank 4109
Sunnycliffs 3496
Sunnyside 4416
Sunnyside 6256
Sunnyside 7305
Sunrise Beach 4567
Sunset 4825
Sunset Beach 6530
Sunshine 2264
Sunshine 3020
Sunshine Acres 4655
Sunshine Bay 2536
Sunshine Beach 4567
Surat 4417
Surf Beach 2536
Surfers Paradise 4217
Surfside 2536

Surges Bay 7116
Surrey Downs 5126
Surrey Hills 3127
Surry Hills 2010
Susan River 4655
Sussex Inlet 2540
Sutherland 1499
Sutherland 2232
Sutherlands 5374
Sutherlands Creek 3331
Sutton 2620
Sutton Forest 2577
Sutton Grange 3448
Suttor 4743
Svensson Heights 4670
Swan Bay 2324
Swan Bay 2471
Swan Bay 7252
Swan Hill 3585
Swan Marsh 3249
Swan Reach 3903
Swan Reach 5354
Swan Vale 2370
Swan View 6056
Swanbourne 6010
Swanhaven 2540
Swanpool 3673
Swans Lagoon 4807
Swansea 2281
Swansea 7190
Swifts Creek 3896
Swinger Hill 2606
Sydenham 2044
Sydenham 3037
Sydney City 2000
Sydney private boxes 2001
Sydney Airport 2020
Sydney Markets 2129

Sylvania 2224
Symonston 2609
Syndal 3149

T
Taabinga 4610
Tabbita 2652
Tabilk 3607
Table Cape 7325
Table Top 2640
Tablelands 4605
Tablelands 4680
Tabulam 2469
Tacoma 2259
Taggerty 3714
Tahlee 2324
Tahmoor 2573
Taigum 4018
Tailem Bend 5260
Tailem Bend private bags 5259
Takalarup 6324
Takilberan 4671
Takone 7325
Talandji 6710
Talbingo 2720
Talbot 3371
Talbot 6302
Taldra 5311
Talegalla Weir 4650
Talgarno 3691
Talgomine 6490
Tallai 4213
Tallangatta 3700
Tallarook 3659
Tallebudgera 4228
Tallegalla 4340
Tallimba 2669
Tallong 2579

Tallwood 2798
Tallygaroopna 3634
Talmalmo 2640
Talwood 4496
Tamala Park 6030
Tamarama 2026
Tambar Springs 2381
Tambellup 6320
Tambo 4478
Tambo Crossing 3893
Tambo Upper 3885
Tamborine 4270
Tamleugh 3669
Tamleugh West 3631
Tammin 6409
Tamworth 2340
Tanah Merah 4128
Tanami 6770
Tanawha 4556
Tanbar 4481
Tanby 4703
Tandarra 3571
Tandegin 6415
Tandora 4650
Tangalooma 4025
Tangambalanga 3691
Tanilba Bay 2319
Tanjil South 3825
Tankerton 3921
Tannum Sands 4680
Tannymorel 4372
Tansey 4601
Tantanoola 5280
Tanunda 5352
Taperoo 5017
Tapitallee 2540
Taplan 5333
Tapping 6065
Tara 4421

Taradale 3447
Tarago 2580
Taragoola 4680
Taralga 2580
Tarana 2787
Taranganba 4703
Taranna 7180
Tarawera 4494
Tarbuck Bay 2428
Tarcoola 5710
Tarcoola Beach 6530
Tarcowie 5431
Tarcutta 2652
Tardun 6628
Taree 2430
Taren Point 2229
Targa 7259
Targinie 4694
Tarin Rock 6353
Taringa 4068
Tarlee 5411
Tarnagulla 3551
Tarneit 3029
Tarong 4615
Taroom 4420
Taroomball 4703
Taroona 7053
Tarpeena 5277
Tarragindi 4121
Tarraleah 7140
Tarramba 4715
Tarranyurk 3414
Tarraville 3971
Tarrawanna 2518
Tarrington 3301
Tarro 2322
Tarwin 3956
Tascott 2250
Tatham 2471

Tathra 2550
Tatong 3673
Tatura 3616
Tatyoon 3378
Taunton 4674
Tawonga 3697
Tawonga South 3698
Tayene 7259
Taylors Arm 2447
Taylors Beach 4850
Taylors Lakes 3038
Te Kowai 4740
Tea Gardens 2324
Tea Tree 7017
Tea Tree Gully 5091
Tecoma 3160
Teddington 4650
Teebar 4620
Teelah 4306
Teesdale 3328
Teesdale 6213
Telangatuk East 3401
Telarah 2320
Telegraph Point 2441
Telfer 6762
Telford 3730
Telina 4680
Tellebang 4630
Telopea 2117
Temora 2666
Tempe 2044
Templers 5371
Templestowe 3106
Templestowe Lower 3107
Tempy 3489
Tenambit 2323
Tenby Point 3984
Tenindewa 6632

Tennant Creek 0860
Tennant Creek private
    bags 0862
Tennant Creek private
    boxes 0861
Tennyson 2754
Tennyson 3572
Tennyson 4105
Tennyson 5022
Tennyson Point 2111
Tenterden 6322
Ienterfield 2372
Teralba 2284
Icrong 3264
Terara 2540
Teringie 5072
Termeil 2539
Terowie 5421
Terranora 2486
Terrey Hills 2084
Terrica 4387
Terrigal 2260
Terry Hie Hie 2400
Teven 2478
Tewantin 4565
Texas 4385
Thabeban 4670
Thagoona 4306
Thallon 4497
Thangool 4716
Tharbogang 2680
Thargomindah 4492
Tharwa 2620
The Basin 2108
The Basin 3154
The Bluff 4340
The Bluff 4355
The Channon 2480
The Common 4701

The Dimonds 4650
The Entrance 2261
The Gap 4061
The Gap 4825
The Gardens 0820
The Gums 4406
The Gurdies 3984
The Hill 2300
The Junction 2291
The Keppels 4700
The Lakes 6556
The Leap 4740
The Levels 5095
The Limits 4825
The Mine 4714
The Monument 4825
The Narrows 0820
The Narrows 4695
The Oaks 2570
The Patch 3792
The Percy Group 4707
The Pines 4357
The Plains 6237
The Range 4700
The Risk 2474
The Rock 2655
The Rocks 2000
The Rocks 2795
The Sisters 3265
The Specatacles 6167
The Summit 4377
The Vines 6069
Thebarton 5031
Theodore 2905
Theodore 4719
Thevenard 5690
Thevenard Island 6711
Thinoomba 4650
Thirlmere 2572

Thirlstane 7307
Thirroul 2515
Thomaston 3074
Thompson Point 4702
Thomson Brook 6239
Thoona 3726
Thoopara 4800
Thora 2454
Thornbury 3071
Thorneside 4158
Thorngate 5082
Thornlands 4164
Thornleigh 2120
Thornlie 6108
Thornlie 6988
Thornton 2322
Thornton 3712
Thornville 4352
Thorpdale 3835
Thorpdale South 3824
Thowgla Valley 3707
Thredbo Village 2625
Three Bridges 3797
Three Hummock Island
    7330
Three Moon 4630
Three Springs 6519
Throssell 6401
Thulimbah 4376
Thumb Creek 2447
Thurgoona 2640
Thuringowa Central 4817
Thursday Island 4875
Ti Tree 0872
Tiaro 4650
Tiberias 7120
Tibooburra 2880
Tibradden 6532
Tichborne 2870

Tidal River 3960
Tieri 4709
Tighes Hill 2297
Tilba Tilba 2546
Tilpa 2840
Timboon 3268
Tin Can Bay 4580
Tinamba 3859
Tinana 4650
Tinaroo 4872
Tinbeerwah 4563
Tincurrin 6361
Tindal RAAF 0853
Tinderbox 7054
Tingalpa 4173
Tingha 2369
Tingira Heights 2290
Tingledale 6333
Tingoora 4608
Tingun 4455
Tinonee 2430
Tinpot 2546
Tintaldra 3708
Tintenbar 2478
Tintinara 5266
Tipton 4405
Tirroan 4671
Tivoli 4305
Tiwi 0810
Tocal 4730
Tocumwal 2714
Togari 7330
Toiberry 7301
Toko 4829
Tolga 4882
Toll 4820
Tolland 2650
Tolmans Hill 7007
Tom Price 6751

Tomago 2322
Tomahawk 7262
Tomakin 2537
Tomerong 2540
Tomingley 2869
Toms Creek 2446
Tonebridge 6244
Tongala 3621
Tonganah 7260
Tonimbuk 3815
Tooheah 4498
Tooborac 3522
Toodyay 6566
Toogong 2864
Toogoolawah 4313
Toolakea 4818
Toolamba 3614
Toolangi 3777
Toolara Forest 4570
Toolern Vale 3337
Tooleybuc 2736
Toolibin 6312
Toolijooa 2534
Toolleen 3551
Toolonda 3401
Toolong 3285
Toolooa 4680
Tooma 2642
Toombul 4012
Toompup 6336
Toondahra 4625
Toongabbie 2146
Toongabbie 3856
Toonumbar 2474
Toora 3962
Tooradin 3980
Toorak 3142
Toorak Gardens 5065
Tooraweenah 2831

Toorbul 4510
Toormina 2452
Toorooka 2440
Tootgarook 3941
Toowong 4066
Toowoomba 4350
Toowoomba private
  boxes 4352
Toowoon Bay 2261
Top Camp 4350
Torbanlea 4662
Torbay 6330
Torndirrup 6330
Toronto 2283
Torquay 3228
Torquay 4655
Torrens 2607
Torrens Creek 4816
Torrens Park 5062
Torrensville 5031
Torrington 2371
Torrumbarry 3562
Tottenham 2873
Tottenham 3012
Toukley 2263
Towamba 2550
Tower Hill 3282
Towers Hill 4820
Town Common 4810
Townsendale 6311
Townson 4341
Townsville 4810
Townview 4825
Towong 3707
Towradgi 2518
Towrang 2580
Trafalgar 3824
Trafalgar 6431
Trangie 2823

Tranmere 5073
Tranmere 7018
Traralgon 3844
Travancore 3032
Travellers Rest 7250
Trawalla 3373
Trawool 3660
Trayning 6488
Treeton 6284
Tregeagle 2480
Tregear 2770
Trent 6333
Trentham 3458
Tresco 3583
Trevallyn 2421
Trevallyn 7250
Trewilga 2869
Triabunna 7190
Trida 2878
Trigg 6029
Trigwell 6393
Trihi 5279
Trinity Beach 4879
Trinity Gardens 5068
Trinity Park 4879
Trott Park 5158
Trotter Creek 4714
Trowutta 7330
Truganina 3029
Trunding 4874
Trundle 2875
Trungley Hall 2666
Trunkey Creek 2795
Truro 5356
Tuan Forest 4650
Tuart Hill 6060
Tuart Hill private boxes
  6939
Tubbut 3888

Tucabia 2462
Tuckurimba 2480
Tuen 4490
Tuena 2583
Tuerong 3915
Tuggerah 2259
Tuggeranong 2900
Tuggeranong private
  boxes 2901
Tuggerawong 2259
Tugun 4224
Tulendeena 7260
Tullah 7321
Tullamarine 3043
Tullamore 2874
Tullibigeal 2669
Tully 4854
Tullymorgan 2463
Tumbarumba 2653
Tumbi Umbi 2261
Tumblong 2729
Tumbulgum 2490
Tumby Bay 5605
Tummaville 4352
Tumoulin 4872
Tumut 2720
Tunbridge 7120
Tuncester 2480
Tuncuny 2428
Tungamah 3728
Tungamull 4702
Tungkillo 5236
Tunnack 7120
Tunnel 7254
Tunstall Square 3109
Tura Beach 2548
Turallin 4357
Turill 2850
Turkey Hill 6426

Turlinjah 2537
Turner 2612
Turners Beach 7315
Turners Marsh 7267
Turondale 2795
Tuross Head 2537
Turramurra 2074
Turrawan 2390
Turrawulla 4742
Turrella 2205
Turvey Park 2650
Tusmore 5065
Tutunup 6280
Tweed Heads 2485
Twelve Mile 2850
Twelve Mile Creek 2324
Twin Waters 4564
Two Rocks 6037
Two Wells 5501
Tyabb 3913
Tyagarah 2481
Tyalgum 2484
Tyenna 7140
Tyers 3844
Tylden 3444
Tynong 3813
Tyrendarra 3285
Tyringham 2453
Tysons Reef 3550

U

Uarbry 2329
Ubobo 4680
Ucarty 6462
Ucarty West 6460
Uduc 6220
Uki 2484
Ulamambri 2357
Ulan 2850

Ularring 6436
Uleybury 5114
Ulladulla 2539
Ullina 3364
Ulmarra 2462
Ulogie 4702
Ulong 2450
Ultima 3544
Ultimo 2007
Ulverstone 7315
Umbakumba 0822
Umbiram 4352
Umina Beach 2257
Unanderra 2526
Undera 3629
Underbool 3509
Underdale 5032
Underwood 4119
Underwood 7268
Ungarie 2669
Ungarra 5607
University of Adelaide
  5005
University of Canberra
  2617
University of Melbourne
  3010
University of New
  England 2351
University of Sydney
  2006
University of Queensland
  4072
University of Tasmania
  7005
University of Wollongong
  2522
University of New South
  Wales 1466

University of New South
Wales 2052
Unley 5061
Upper Barron 4883
Upper Bowman 2422
Upper Brookfield 4069
Upper Capel 6239
Upper Castra 7315
Upper Coomera 4209
Upper Daradgee 4860
Upper Dawson 4454
Upper Esk /214
Upper Ferntree Gully 3156
Upper Flagstone 4344
Upper Glastonbury 4570
Upper Haughton 4809
Upper Hermitage 5131
Upper Horton 2347
Upper Kandanga 4570
Upper Kedron 4055
Upper Lansdowne 2430
Upper Lockyer 4352
Upper Mount Gravatt
4122
Upper Murray 6390
Upper Myall 2423
Upper Orara 2450
Upper Plenty 3756
Upper Rouchel 2336
Upper Stone 4850
Upper Sturt 5156
Upper Swan 6059
Upper Tenthill 4343
Upper Warren 6258
Upper Woodstock 7150
Upper Yarraman 4614
Upwey 3158
Uraidla 5142
Uralba 2477

Uralla 2358
Urana 2645
Urangan 4655
Urangeline East 2656
Uranquinty 2652
Urbenville 2475
Uriarra 2611
Urisino 2840
Urraween 4655
Urrbrae 5064
Urunga 2455
Useless Loop 6537
Usher 6230
Utakarra 6530
Utchee Creek 4871
Uxbridge 7140

V

Vacy 2421
Vale Park 5081
Vale View 4358
Valencia Creek 3860
Valentine 2280
Valentine 6532
Valkyrie 4742
Valla Beach 2448
Valley Heights 2777
Valley View 5093
Vancouver Peninsula
6330
Varley 6355
Varroville 2566
Varsity Lakes 4227
Vasa Views 4860
Vasey 3407
Vasse 6280
Vaucluse 2030
Veitch 5312
Ventnor 4630

Venus Bay 3956
Venus Bay 5607
Veradilla 4347
Verdun 5245
Vergemont 4730
Verges Creek 2440
Vermont 3133
Verona Sands 7112
Vervale 3814
Victor Harbor 5211
Victoria Hill 4361
Victoria Park 6100
Victoria Park private
boxes 6979
Victoria Plains 4751
Victoria Plantation 4850
Victoria Point 4165
Victoria River Downs
0852
Victoria Rock 6429
Victoria Valley 3294
Victoria Valley 7140
Victory Heights 6432
Viewbank 3084
Villawood 2163
Vincent 4814
Vincentia 2540
Vinegar Hill 4343
Vineyard 2765
Vinifera 3591
Violet Town 3669
Virginia 0835
Virginia 4014
Virginia 5120
Vista 5091
Vittoria 2799
Vittoria 6230
Viveash 6056
Voyager Point 2172

W

W Tree 3885
Waaia 3637
Wacol 4076
Wadbilliga 2546
Waddamana 7030
Wadderin 6369
Waddington 6509
Waddy Forest 6515
Wadeye 0822
Wael 6407
Wagaman 0810
Wagerup 6215
Wagga Wagga 2650
Wagga Wagga RAAF
2651
Waggrakine 6530
Wagin 6315
Wahgunyah 3687
Wahoon 4625
Wahring 3608
Wahroonga 2076
Waikerie 5330
Waikiki 6169
Wainui 4404
Wairewa 3887
Wairuna 4872
Waitara 2077
Waitchie 3544
Wakefield 2278
Wakeley 2176
Wakerley 4154
Wakool 2710
Walbundrie 2642
Walcha 2354
Walebing 6510
Walgett 2832
Walgoolan 6422
Walhalla 3825

Walkamin 4872
Walkaway 6528
Walkers Point 4650
Walkerston 4751
Walkervale 4670
Walkerville 3956
Walkerville 5081
Walkerville South 3956
Walkley Heights 5098
Walla Walla 2659
Wallabadah 2343
Wallace 3352
Wallacia 2745
Wallaga Lake 2546
Wallan 3756
Wallangarra 4383
Wallangra 2360
Wallarah 2259
Wallareenya 6721
Wallarobba 2420
Wallaroo 4702
Wallaroo 5556
Wallaroo 6429
Wallaroo Mines 5554
Wallaville 4671
Wallendbeen 2588
Wallerawang 2845
Walliebum 4655
Walligan 4655
Wallington 3221
Walliston 6076
Walloon 4306
Wallsend 2287
Wallumbilla 4428
Wallup 3401
Walmer 2820
Walmsley 6330
Walmul 4714
Walpa 3875

Walpeup 3507
Walpole 6398
Walsall 6280
Walter Lever Estate 4856
Walwa 3709
Walyormouring 6460
Walyurin 6363
Wamberal 2260
Wamboin 2620
Wambool 2795
Wamenusking 6383
Wamoon 2705
Wamuran 4512
Wanaaring 2840
Wanalta 3612
Wanbi 5310
Wandal 4700
Wandana 6532
Wandana Heights 3216
Wandandian 2540
Wandella 2550
Wandering 6308
Wandi 6167
Wandiligong 3744
Wandillup 6256
Wandin Norht 3139
Wandina 6530
Wando Vale 3312
Wandoan 4419
Wandong 3758
Wandsworth 2365
Wanerie 6503
Wang Wauk 2423
Wangan 4871
Wanganella 2710
Wangara 6065
Wangaratta 3677
Wangaratta private
   boxes 3676

Wangaratta 4806
Wangary 5607
Wangi Wangi 2267
Wangoom 3279
Wanguri 0810
Wanilla 5607
Wanjuru 4860
Wannamal 6505
Wannanup 6210
Wanneroo 6065
Wanneroo private boxes
   6946
Wanniassa 2903
Wansbrough 6320
Wantirna 3152
Wantirna South 3152
Wapengo 2550
Warabrook 2304
Waramanga 2611
Warana 4575
Waratah 2298
Waratah 7321
Waratah Bay 3959
Waratah West 2298
Warawarrup 6220
Warburton 3799
Warburton 4823
Wardell 2477
Wardering 6311
Warding East 6405
Wards River 2422
Wareek 3465
Wareemba 2046
Warenda 4829
Warialda 2402
Warilla 2528
Warkworth 2330
Warmun 6743
Warnbro 6169

Warncoort 3243
Warneet 3980
Warner 4500
Warner Glen 6288
Warners Bay 2282
Warnervale 2259
Warnoah 4718
Warnung 4605
Warooka 5577
Waroona 6215
Warra 4411
Warrachie 5607
Warrachuppin 6423
Warracknabeal 3393
Warradale 5046
Warradarge 6518
Warragamba 2752
Warragul 3820
Warrah Creek 2339
Warrak 3377
Warramboo 5650
Warrandyte 3113
Warrandyte South 3134
Warrane 7018
Warranwood 3134
Warrawee 2074
Warrawong 2502
Warrego 0862
Warrell Creek 2447
Warren 2824
Warrenbayne 3670
Warrenheip 3352
Warrenup 6330
Warriewood 2102
Warrimoo 2774
Warringah Mall 2100
Warrion 3249
Warriwillah 2429
Warrnambool 3280

Warroo 4387
Warrow 5607
Warrubullen 4871
Warrumbungle 2828
Warwick 4370
Warwick 6024
Warwick Farm 2170
Washpool 2425
Washpool 4309
Wasleys 5400
Watalgan 4670
Watanobbi 2259
Watchem 3482
Watchupga 3485
Wateranga 4621
Waterbank 6725
Watercarrin 6407
Waterfall 2233
Waterfall Gully 5066
Waterford 4133
Waterford 6152
Waterford West 4133
Waterfront Place 4001
Waterhouse 7262
Waterloo 2017
Waterloo 4673
Waterloo 6228
Waterloo 7109
Waterloo Corner 5110
Watermans Bay 6020
Watervale 5452
Waterview Heights 2460
Waterways 3195
Watheroo 6513
Watson 2602
Watsonia 3087
Watsons Bay 2030
Watsons Creek 2355
Watsons Creek 3097

Watsons Crossing 4385
Watsonville 4887
Wattamolla 2535
Wattamondara 2794
Wattening 6568
Wattle Camp 4615
Wattle Flat 2795
Wattle Glen 3096
Wattle Grove 2173
Wattle Grove 4610
Wattle Grove 6107
Wattle Grove 7109
Wattle Hill 7172
Wattle Park 3128
Wattle Park 5066
Wattle Ridge 4357
Wattlebank 4704
Wattleup 6166
Wattoning 6479
Waubra 3352
Wauchope 2446
Waurn Ponds 3216
Wavell Heights 4012
Waverley 2024
Waverley 4825
Waverley 7250
Waverton 2060
Wayatinah 7140
Wayville 5034
Weatherboard 3352
Webb 4860
Webberton 6530
Wedderburn 3518
Wedderburn 2560
Wedge Island 6044
Wedgecarrup 6315
Wedgefield 6721
Wee Jasper 2582
Wee Waa 2388

Weegena 7304
Weengallon 4497
Weering 3251
Weerriba 4703
Weetah 7304
Weetaliba 2395
Weetangera 2614
Weethalle 2669
Weetulta 5573
Weilmoringle 2839
Weipa 4874
Weir River 4406
Welbungin 6577
Welby 2575
Welcome Creek 4670
Weld Range 6640
Weldborough 7264
Welland 5007
Wellard 6170
Wellcamp 4350
Wellers Hill 4121
Wellesley 6233
Wellington 2820
Wellington 5259
Wellington Forest 6236
Wellington Mill 6236
Wellington Point 4160
Wellstead 6328
Welsby 4507
Welshpool 3966
Welshpool 6106
Wembley 6014
Wembley private boxes
  6913
Wembley Downs 6019
Wendoree Park 2250
Wendouree 3355
Wendouree Village 3355
Wengenville 4615

Wentworth 2648
Wentworth Falls 2782
Wentworthville 2145
Werneth 3352
Werombi 2570
Werri Beach 2534
Werribee 3030
Werrimull 3496
Werrington 2747
Werris Creek 2341
Wesburn 3799
Wesley Vale 7307
West Armidale 2350
West Ballidu 6606
West Bathurst 2795
West Beach 5024
West Beach 6450
West Binnu 6532
West Burleigh 4219
West Busselton 6280
West Cape Howe 6330
West Casuarinas 6630
West Chatswood 1515
West Coolup 6214
West Croydon 5008
West Devonport 7310
West End 4101
West End 4810
West End 6530
West Fitzgerald 6337
West Footscray 3012
West Gladstone 4680
West Gosford 2250
West Haldon 4359
West Haven 2443
West Hindmarsh 5007
West Hobart 7000
West Holleton 6369
West Hoxton 2171

West Ipswich 4305
West Island Cocos
  (Keeling) Islands 6799
West Kalgoorlie 6430
West Lakes 5021
West Lakes Shore 5020
West Lamington 6430
West Launceston 7250
West Leederville private
  boxes 6901
West Leederville 6007
West Lyons River 6705
West Mackay 4740
West Melbourne 3003
West Pennant Hills 2125
West Perth 6005
West Perth private boxes
  6872
West Pine 7316
West Pingelly 6308
West Pinjarra 6208
West Point 4819
West Popanyinning 6309
West Prairie 4403
West Pymble 2073
West Richmond 5033
West River 6346
West Rockhampton 4700
West Ryde 1685
West Ryde 2114
West Stowe 4680
West Swan 6055
West Tamworth 2340
West Toodyay 6566
West Wallsend 2286
West Wollongong 2500
West Wyalong 2671
Westbourne Park 5041
Westbrook 4350

Westbury 7303
Westcourt 4870
Westdale 2340
Westdale 6304
Western Creek 4357
Western Creek 7304
Western Junction 7212
Westerway 7140
Westfield 6112
Westgate 2048
Westgrove 4454
Westlake 4074
Westleigh 2120
Westmead 2145
Westmeadows 3049
Westmere 3351
Westminster 6061
Weston 2326
Weston 2611
Weston Creek 2611
Westonia 6423
Westwood 4702
Westwood 6316
Westwood 7292
Wetherill Park 2164
Wetheron 4625
Weymouth 7252
Whalan 2770
Whale Beach 2107
Wharminda 5603
Wheatlands 4606
Wheeler Hits 2097
Wheelers Hill 3150
Wherrol Flat 2429
Whetstone 4387
Whian Whian 2480
Whichello 4352
Whim Creek 6718
Whitby 6123

White Cliffs 2836
White Gum Valley 6162
White Hills 3550
White Hills 7258
White Mountain 4352
White Patch 4507
White Peak 6532
White Rock 4868
Whitebridge 2290
Whitefoord 7120
Whiteman 6068
Whitemark 7255
Whitomoro 7303
Whiteside 4503
Whitfield 3733
Whitfield 4870
Whitsunday 4802
Whittaker 6207
Whittington 3219
Whittlesea 3757
Whitton 2705
Whorouly 3735
Whyalla 5600
Whyalla Jenkins 5609
Whyalla Norrie 5608
Whyalla Playford 5600
Whyalla Stuart 5608
Whyte Yarcowie 5420
Wialki 6473
Wiangaree 2474
Wicherina 6532
Wickepin 6370
Wickham 2293
Wickham 6720
Wickliffe 3379
Widgee Crossing 4570
Widgeegoara 4490
Widgelli 2680
Widgiemooltha 6443

Wieambilla 4413
Wights Mountain 4520
Wigton 4612
Wilberforce 2756
Wilberforce 6302
Wilbetree 2850
Wilbinga 6041
Wilby 3728
Wilcannia 2836
Wildes Meadow 2577
Wiley Park 2195
Wilga 6243
Wilgarrup 6258
Wilgoyne 6479
Wilkesdale 4608
Willagee 6156
Willaston 5118
Willaura 3379
Willawarrin 2440
Willawong 4110
Willbriggie 2680
Willetton 6155
Willetton private boxes
    6955
William Bay 6333
Williams 6391
Williamsdale 2620
Williamstown 3016
Williamstown 5351
Williamstown 6430
Williamtown 2318
Williamtown RAAF 2314
Willina 2423
Wilmot 2770
Willoughby 2068
Willow Grove 3825
Willow Tree 2339
Willow Vale 4209
Willowbank 4306

Willows Gemfields 4702
Wills 4829
Willung 3847
Willung South 3844
Willunga 5172
Willyung 6330
Wilmington 5485
Wilmot 7310
Wilson 6107
Wilson Beach 4800
Wilson Valley 4625
Wilsonton 4350
Wilston 4051
Wilton 2571
Wiluna 6646
Wilyabrup 6280
Wimbledon 2795
Winchelsea 3241
Windabout 6450
Windale 2306
Windang 2528
Windaroo 4207
Windermere 3352
Windermere 4670
Windermere 7252
Windeyer 2850
Windeyer 4478
Windorah 4481
Windsor 2756
Windsor 3181
Windsor 4030
Windsor 5501
Windsor Gardens 5087
Winegrove 2460
Wingala 2099
Wingello 2579
Wingen 2337
Wingfield 5013
Wingham 2429

Winkle 5343
Winkleigh 7275
Winmalee 2777
Winnaleah 7265
Winnap 3304
Winnejup 6255
Winnellie 0820
Winnellie private boxes
    0821
Winnellie private bags
    0822
Winslow 3281
Winston 4825
Winston Hills 2153
Wintergarden 4002
Winthrop 6150
Winton 3673
Winton 4735
Winwill 4347
Wirrabara 5481
Wirrimah 2803
Wirrinya 2871
Wirrulla 5661
Wiseleigh 3885
Wisemans Creek 2795
Wisemans Ferry 2775
Wishart 3189
Wishart 4122
Wistow 5251
Witchcliffe 6286
Withcott 4352
Witheren 4275
Withers 6230
Wittenoom 6751
Wittenoom Hills 6447
Wivenhoe 7320
Wivenhoe Hill 4311
Woden 2606
Wodonga 3690

Wodonga private boxes
    3689
Wogolin 6370
Wokalup 6221
Wolffdene 4207
Wollar 2850
Wollert 3750
Wolli Creek 2205
Wollombi 2325
Wollomombi 2350
Wollongbar 2477
Wollongong 2500
Wollongong private
    boxes 2520
Wollstonecraft 2065
Wollun 2354
Wolseley 5269
Wolumla 2550
Womarden 6519
Wombarra 2515
Wombat 2587
Wombelano 3409
Wombeyan Caves 2580
Womboota 2731
Won Wron 3971
Wonbah 4671
Wonboyn 2551
Wondai 4606
Wondalga 2729
Wondalli 4390
Wondecla 4887
Wondunna 4655
Wonga 4873
Wonga Park 3115
Wongabel 4883
Wongaling Beach 4852
Wongamine 6401
Wongan Hills 6603
Wongarbon 2831

Wongarra 3221
Wongawallan 4210
Wongawilli 2530
Wonglepong 4275
Wongoondy 6630
Wonnerup 6280
Wonthaggi 3995
Wonthella 6530
Woocoo 4620
Wood Wood 3596
Woodanilling 6316
Woodberry 2322
Woodbine 2560
Woodbine 4343
Woodbridge 6056
Woodbridge 7162
Woodburn 2472
Woodbury 7120
Woodcroft 2767
Woodcroft 5162
Woodenbong 2476
Woodend 3442
Woodend 4305
Wooderson 4680
Woodfield 3715
Woodford 2463
Woodford 2778
Woodford 3281
Woodford 4514
Woodforde 5072
Woodgate 4660
Woodhill 2535
Woodhouselee 2580
Woodlands 2536
Woodlands 4343
Woodlands 6018
Woodleigh 3945
Woodleigh 4352
Woodleigh Gardens 0812

Woodmillar 4625
Woodridge 4114
Woodridge 6041
Woodrising 2284
Woodroffe 0830
Woods Point 3723
Woodsdale 7120
Woodside 3874
Woodside 5244
Woodstock 2793
Woodstock 3751
Woodstock 4816
Woodstock 7109
Woodstock Un Loddon 3551
Woodstock West 3463
Woodvale 6026
Woodview 2470
Woodville 2321
Woodville 5011
Woodville Gardens 5012
Woodville North 5012
Woodwark 4802
Woody Point 4019
Woogenellup 6324
Wool Bay 5575
Wool Wool 3249
Woolamai 3995
Woolbrook 2354
Woolein 4702
Woolgoolga 2456
Woolgorong 6630
Wooli 2462
Woollahra 1350
Woollahra 2025
Woollamia 2540
Woolloomooloo 2011
Woolloongabba 4102
Woolmer 4352

Woolner 0820
Woolnorth 7330
Woolocutty 6369
Woolomin 2340
Woolooga 4570
Woolooma 2337
Woolooware 2230
Wooloowin 4030
Woolshed Flat 3518
Woolsthorpe 3276
Woolwich 2110
Woomargama 2644
Woombye 4559
Woomelang 3485
Woomera 5720
Woondul 4357
Woongarrah 2259
Woongoolba 4207
Woonona 2517
Woorabinda 4713
Wooragee 3747
Wooramel 6701
Woori Yallock 3139
Woorim 4507
Woorinen 3589
Woorinen South 3588
Woorndoo 3272
Wooroloo 6558
Wooroolin 4608
Wooroona 4702
Wooroonden 4605
Wooroonooran 4860
Woorree 6530
Wootha 4552
Woottating 6562
Wootton 2423
Woowoonga 4621
Woree 4868
World Square 2002

World Trade Centre 3005
Worongary 4213
Woronora 2232
Woronora Heights 2233
Worrigee 2540
Worsley 6225
Wowan 4702
Woy Woy 2256
Wrattens Forest 4601
Wrights Beach 2540
Wrights Creek 4869
Wubin 6612
Wudinna 5652
Wulagi 0812
Wulgulmerang 3885
Wulguru 4811
Wulkuraka 4305
Wundowie 6560
Wunghnu 3635
Wungong 6112
Wunjunga 4806
Wura 4714
Wuraming 6390
Wurdiboluc 3241
Wurruk 3850
Wurtulla 4575
Wuruma Dam 4627
Wutul 4352
Wy Yung 3875
Wyaga 4390
Wyalkatchem 6485
Wyalla 4615
Wyalong 2671
Wyandra 4489
Wybong 2333
Wycarbah 4702
Wycheproof 3527
Wychitella 3525
Wye River 3221

Wyee 2259
Wyena 7254
Wyening 6568
Wylie Creek 2372
Wynarka 5306
Wyndham 2550
Wyndham 6740
Wyndham Vale 3024
Wynn Vale 5127
Wynnum 4178
Wynyard 7325
Wyola 6407
Wyoming 2250
Wyong 2259
Wyongah 2259
Wyrallah 2480
Wyreema 4352
Wyuna 3620

X

Xantippe 6609

Y

Yaamba 4704
Yaapeet 3424
Yabba North 3646
Yabberup 6239
Yabulu 4818
Yacka 5470
Yackandandah 3749
Yagaburne 4390
Yagoona 2199
Yahl 5291
Yakamia 6330
Yalangur 4352
Yalata 5690
Yalbraith 2580
Yalgoo 6635
Yallabatharra 6535

Yallah 2530
Yallambic 3085
Yallingup 6282
Yallourn North 3825
Yalwal 2540
Yalyalup 6280
Yamanto 4305
Yamba 2464
Yambuk 3285
Yambuna 3621
Yan Yean 3755
Yanac 3418
Yanakie 3960
Yanchep 6035
Yanco 2703
Yandanooka 6522
Yandaran 4673
Yandarlo 4478
Yanderra 2574
Yandilla 4352
Yandina 4561
Yandoit 3461
Yandoo Creek 6701
Yangan 4371
Yangebup 6164
Yaninee 5653
Yankalilla 5203
Yanmah 6258
Yannarie 6710
Yannathan 3981
Yantabulla 2840
Yaouk 2629
Yaraka 4702
Yarawindah 6509
Yarck 3719
Yardarino 6525
Yargullen 4401
Yarloop 6218
Yaroomba 4573

Yarra 2580
Yarra Glen 3775
Yarra Junction 3797
Yarrabah 4871
Yarragadee 6522
Yarragon 3823
Yarralumla 2600
Yarram 3971
Yarramalong 2259
Yarraman 4614
Yarrambat 3091
Yarramundi 2753
Yarranlea 4356
Yarraville 3013
Yarrawalla 3575
Yarrawarrah 2233
Yarrawonga 0830
Yarrawonga 2850
Yarrawonga 3730
Yarrawonga Park 2264
Yarrol 4630
Yarroweyah 3644
Yarrunga 2577
Yarrunga 3677
Yarwun 4694
Yass 2582
Yatala 4207
Yatala Vale 5126
Yathroo 6507
Yattalunga 2251
Yatte Yattah 2539
Yea 3717
Yeal 6503
Yealering 6372
Yeelanna 5632
Yeerongpilly 4105
Yelarbon 4388
Yelbeni 6487
Yelgun 2483

Yellingbo 3139
Yellow Rock 2777
Yellowdine 6426
Yelta 5558
Yelverton 6280
Yenda 2681
Yenda 4625
Yendon 3352
Yengarie 4650
Yennora 2161
Yeo 3249
Yeodene 3249
Yeoval 2868
Yeppoon 4703
Yerecoin 6571
Yerong Creek 2642
Yeronga 4104
Yerrinbool 2575
Yetholme 2795
Yetman 2410
Yetna 6532
Yilkari 6430
Yilliminning 6312
Yimbun 4313
Yinnar 3869
Yirrkala 0880
Yoganup 6275
Yokine 6060
Yolla 7325
Yongala 5493
Yoogali 2680
Yoongarillup 6280
York 6302
York Plains 7120
Yorketown 5576
Yorkeys Knob 4878
Yorkrakine 6409
Yornaning 6311
Yornup 6256

Yoting 6383
Youanmite 3646
Youndegin 6407
Young 2584
Youngs Siding 6330
Youngtown 7249
Yourdamung Lake 6225
Yowah 4490
Yowie Bay 2228
Yowrie 2550
Yuendumu 0872
Yugar 4520
Yulabilla 4416
Yulara 0872
Yuleba 4427
Yumali 5261
Yuna 6532
Yundool 3727
Yungaburra 4884
Yunta 5440
Yuroke 3063

Z
Zanthus 6434
Zeehan 7469
Zetland 2017
Zillmere 4034
Zilzie 4710
Zuytdorp 6536